IT HAPPENED IN
NEW YORK

By Fran Capo and Frank Borzellieri

Illustrated by Lisa Harvey

TWODOT

Helena, Montana

To my mom, Rose; my sister, Sharon; my son, Spencer;
and in loving memory of my dad, Frank
—Fran

To my nephew, Timmy
—Frank

A · TWODOT · BOOK

Falcon® is continually expanding its list of regional history books. You can order extra copies of this book and get information and prices for other Falcon® books by writing to Falcon, P.O. Box 1718, Helena, MT 59624 or calling 1-800-582-2665. Please ask for a free copy of our current catalog listing all TwoDot® books. Visit our website at www.Falcon.com or contact us by e-mail at falcon@falcon.com.

© 2000 Falcon® Publishing, Inc., Helena, Montana.
TwoDot® is an imprint of Falcon® Publishing, Inc.
Printed in the United States of America.

1 2 3 4 5 6 7 8 9 0 BP 05 04 03 02 01 00

Cover art and inside illustrations © 2000 Lisa Harvey

Falcon® Publishing gratefully acknowledges Clifton Hood, Associate Professor of History, Hobart and William Smith Colleges, for reviewing this manuscript for historical accuracy.

Library of Congress Cataloging-in-Publication Data

Capo, Fran, 1959-
    It happened in New York/Fran Capo, Frank Borzellieri
        p. cm.
    ISBN 1056044-899-7
        1. New York (N.Y.)—History—Anecdotes. I. Borzellieri, Frank. II. Title.

F128.36. C36 2000
974.7'1—dc21   99-089601

Acknowledgments

Like children on an Easter egg hunt, bit by bit we uncovered facts in New York history to bring to you in our chapters. We were looking for little-known facts—facts that would make you go "Wow, I didn't know that." We wanted to bring you history in a way that you would remember and hopefully pass along to your kids. Unfortunately, it wasn't always so easy to find. Digging requires work, but there were many hunters along the way who helped us on our quest—each giving us a piece of the puzzle and leading us closer to our find.

Where it all began:

•Thanks to William C. Smith, a fellow writer who sent the notice over the internet to Fran through our writing group, Writerslink, about the writing opportunity with TwoDot Books.

•Thanks to Charlene Patterson, our dear editor who accepted the idea of doing a "It Happened in New York" book when she was looking for a western state. Without your "Yes," none of the other thank yous would have been possible. We're sure our persistence helped a little . . . come on.

•Special thanks to William Asadorian, librarian at the Central Queens Library, who always smiled when he saw us coming and even complimented us indirectly by thinking we were students working on a school paper.

•Special thanks to Judy Gordon, librarian at the Bayside Branch of the Queens Library, who always enthusiastically wanted to know what chapter we were "working on now." She even suggested a children's version of *It Happened in New York*. Hear that Charlene?

•Special thanks to Barry Moreno, librarian at the Liberty Museum, who spent one hour on the phone telling us all sorts of interesting and little-known facts about the Statue of Liberty.

•Thanks to *Niagara Gazette* reporter Don Glynn who sent us and trusted us, complete strangers, with his copy of an out-of-circulation brochure on the drying up of Niagara Falls and gave us an eyewitness account of what it was like to walk upon the dried-up falls.

•Thanks to Roxanne Kaplan, wife and co-author with her husband Stephen Kaplan of *The Amityville Horror Conspiracy*, who provided enlightening anecdotes for "The Amityville Horror" chapter.

•Thanks to Patrick E. McCarthy for his in-depth knowledge of searching the internet.

•Thanks to Bobby Casulli, Jr. and Andy Revele for their help searching the web for P.T. Barnum.

•Thanks to fellow Writerslink writer Gary Lehman who led Fran to David Minor and his fabulous timetable of history website at http://home.eznet.net/~dminor.

•Thanks to David Minor who led us to Jim Dierks, who runs the New York Museum of Transportation located on the East River at Town Line in the town of Rush, in West Henrietta, New York, for taking the time to photocopy then send us eyewitness accounts and information on the DeWitt Clinton.

•Thanks to Marion O'Keefe, the weekend manager and historian at the Barnum Musuem in Bridgeport, Conneticut, who gave us a grand individual tour. Thanks also to Barbara Alberts who led us to curator Kathy Keefer, who told us around what date in the newspaper to track down the Brooklyn Bridge story.

•Thanks to Dick Anders, historian at the New York State Library, for information on the forged Manhattan deed, and to Dr. Charles Gehring, who has vast information on the Netherland Project in Albany on his website http://www.nnp.org.

•Thanks to Calbrini Hospice nurse Betty Monohan, who suggested the Amityville Horror as the subject of one of our chapters, and who was so helpful and caring with Fran's dad.

•Thanks to Ashrita Furman, who suggested the "Stolen Star" chapter and told us where to find information on it.

•Thanks to the New-York Historical Society and all its librarians who helped us on many occasions. Special thanks to Mariam Touba and Alice Gingold.

•Thanks to Sandra at the Albany Institute of History and Art for faxing over detailed information on the Dewitt Clinton, and who didn't care if her name was mentioned as long as the institute was.

•Thanks to the reference specialists at the New York State History Museum who faxed us information on the Dewitt Clinton as well.

•Thanks to the guys in the Long Island Room at the Central Queens library for recognizing Frank and liking his columns, as well as for copying endless pages out of reference books we couldn't take out.

The Untold Heroes:

There were some chapters that were cut out from the book after research was done, either because they didn't happen in New York or because there wasn't enough "juicy" stuff. But nonetheless there were individuals who gave their time and energy for the initial research and they should not go unmentioned.

•Thanks to Nan Hyland of the Mann Library at Cornell University for faxing parts of an out-of-print agricultural handbook for the Japanese Beetle Invasion chapter. Unfortunately it happened in New Jersey.

•Thanks to historian Burns Patterson of the historic Hudson Valley for all his tales of Sleepy Hollow. And thanks to Ann Marie at the Chamber of Commerce, and Mary Ann Marshall of the Historical Society in Sleepy Hollow as well. If only there was a real ghost, guys, we could have used this chapter.

Last but never least:

From Fran:

•Thanks to my mom, Rose; sister Sharon; dad Frank; and son Spencer for constantly being enthused about the book and for understanding the little time that I could spend with them during this project.

•Thanks to my 9th grade typing teacher who told me one day I would need to know how to type fast . . . you were right.

From Frank:

•Thanks to my editor at the *Leader-Observer* newspaper chain, Walter Sanchez, who tolerated my frequent journeys into cyberspace to research material for this book.

Contents

The Purchase of Manhattan for the Price of a Cheap Pair of Sneakers
· 1626 ·

The ship slowly pulled up to the shores of New Amsterdam as two hundred settlers and their appointed governor, Peter Minuit, gazed at their new homeland. It was May 4, 1626 when Minuit first set foot on New York soil—a land that according to legend had been occupied by man for five thousand years. Human bones dug up at various sites many years later confirmed that different groups of migrating Indians had climbed over the grassy mountains, plains and forests, and some had made their homes along these very river banks.

Minuit had been sent in as a reinforcement by the head honchos of the Dutch West India Company. This company had formed in 1621, for the purpose of governing and establishing a permanent colony in the New World. When the Europeans first discovered this land, they wanted to claim it. One of the first countries to do so was The Netherlands. The Dutch wanted to make as much money as possible in the New World. They were commercial-minded and started to trade with the local Indians. (One of the hot items of the time was beaver pelts.) They also wanted to expand trade between West Africa and New Foundland. They thought by establishing a permanent American colony they could reach this goal.

Prior to Minuit's arrival, The Dutch West India Company had sent Cornelius May and thirty Walloon (French-speaking refugees from Flanders, which is now Belgium) families to start a new colony. They were given very specific instructions: spread out to claim as large an area as they could from Manhattan Island to what is now known as Hartford, Connecticut. They were on a mission. The Walloons were ordered not to trade with the Indians. They were told to set up farming and industry. They made only slow progress, but a lot of the cash seemed to find its way mysteriously into Cornelius May's pockets.

Minuit's job was to clean up the mess that the previous governors, the incompetent and unsavory May and William Verhulst, had created. Being a shrewd and fair businessman, Minuit wanted to find a way to increase profits for the corporation by guarding its monopoly of the fur trade and by being dedicated to the people, but also by staying on good terms with the friendly Indians.

His jobs were to fight off foreign enemies and domestic troubles, be on guard for Indian attacks, watch for border aggression, oversee the elaborate trading regulations that the Dutch West India Company followed, and then review every single administrative decision. But like any job, the directors in The Netherlands could override any of his decisions, especially if the colonists started to complain.

After just a few days, it was obvious to Minuit that Manhattan Island was the best place to establish a central government site for the colony. Location, location, location. He then did what any good governor would do. He decided to buy Manhattan Island for his people. Within three weeks of his arrival, he sauntered up to some Carnarsie Indians and cleverly convinced them to sell him twenty-two square miles of Manhattan Island for the price of a cheap pair of sneakers: sixty guilders, or $23.70. He was determined, and he truly believed he had treated the Indians fairly. He had cut the real estate deal of the millennium. Too bad he wasn't making a commission. Manhattan today is worth well over sixty billion dollars. Not bad for a new governor off the boat.

The Dutch West India Company reported to the government in the Netherlands about Minuit's purchase in a letter dated Nov. 5, 1626.

> High Mighty Sirs:
> Here arrived yesterday the Ship *The Arms of Amsterdam* which sailed from New Netherland out of the Mauritius (Hudson) River on September 23; they report that our people there are of good courage and live peaceably. Their women, also have borne children there, they have bought the island Manhattan from the wild men for the value of sixty guilders, is of 11,000 morgens in extent. [A morgen equals about 2 acres.]

Everyone was thrilled. There was only one problem. Minuit had purchased the island from the wrong Indians. The Indians that he so easily convinced to sell the land didn't even own it. The Carnarsie Indians were mainly based out of Long Island. They were simply heading west to a summer camping place where they could fish and enjoy the season. Minuit approached them, offered to trade with them for the land, and they gladly thought, "sure, why not." Then they continued on their way, but now only richer. Minuit was happy, thinking he had made the deal so swiftly, when in fact he had just bought land from people who didn't own it. The land should have been purchased from the Wappingers, an Algonquin tribe, who were the rightful owners of Manhattan Island. The Wappingers sold the Dutch another parcel of earth— the Bronx and Westchester County.

Either way, the Dutch claim to Manhattan was never disputed, and Minuit was still credited with a great purchase. Minuit built up Manhattan Island. He recalled some of the Walloons to settle at the tip and established a planned town of about 270 people complete with forts, homes, farms and government buildings.

Minuit was called home in 1631, after he and a minister did not see eye to eye on some issues. He was unwilling to halt private fur trade, something that a lot of the settlers secretly made money on.

He never realized just how shrewd a shopper he had been. Too bad he didn't hold onto his receipt for proof. No deed of the sale survives today—it is not known if there ever was one—but a clever fake is forever archived in the state files in Albany.

It Started Over
a Peach
· 1655 ·

Looking out his townhouse window, fierce-tempered, peg-legged Governor Peter Stuyvesant gazed upon his village. He lived in the tallest of New Amsterdam's three hundred homes. He could see across the main canal to the north to City Hall, the main hub of colony activity. Near the end of the canal were the poorhouses that the deacons of the Dutch church took care of. The city gallows could be seen at the southern end of the island.

Small, quaint, cozy houses lined Broadway Street to the end of the village. Farmhouses began where the homes ended. Many colonists chose rugged farm life rather than the hustle and bustle of the city. Windmills and flower gardens sprinkled among the houses reminded the settlers of their homeland in The Netherlands. The Dutch West India Company, the largest company at the time, had separate gardens of fruits and vegetables to provide for its seventy-five employees.

As Stuyvesant looked west he could see the town's burying grounds tucked between the homes of two local residents, Dirck Wiggerts and Hendrick Van Dyck, a former town sheriff.

Mr. Van Dyck's farm was located near a steep dirt road called Beaver's Path, which ran down to the riverbank. It was near the corner of Broadway and today's Wall Street. This was the gateway into town for the sailors, visitors, and Indians arriving by canoe.

Like most of the townfolk, Mr. Van Dyck did not like the Indians, and the feeling was mutual among some of the Indian tribes. But all of the colonists relied heavily on their Indian neighbors for food, trade, and to sell them land. Some Indians were friendly and would help the settlers fight against the Indians that were hostile.

A lot of fighting also occurred between the Dutch and the Swedish who had settled in the same area. New Amsterdam's and New Sweden's claims to land had not yet been settled.

Looking over his town, Stuyvesant made a decision. He had to get rid of the Swedish competition along the Delaware River to restore some peace to his people. So in the middle of the night, he led six hundred of his men in seven ships to the center of New Sweden. He captured two of their forts. Proudly, he sailed home with the good news for the colonists.

As Stuyvesant was singing on his ship, feeling victorious, a young Indian girl was smelling the wonderful scent of ripe peaches in Mr. Van Dyck's orchard. It was the calm day of September 15, 1655 when she strolled along the street and decided to pick a few peaches. As she was biting on the sweet forbidden fruit, Van Dyck spotted her. In his anger, he picked up a gun and shot the young girl dead. Her body slumped beneath a peach tree with the deadly peach half-eaten in her hand.

When she did not return home, her family came to search for her. They found her body and carried it back to their home. That night word spread among the Indian tribes. The Mahicans,

Pachamis, Esopus, and Hackensack Indians joined forces in a surprise attack on Manhattan. Five hundred angry Indians approached New Amsterdam along the Hudson River with revenge in their hearts. They ransacked many Dutch homes, smashing furniture and ripping up bed sheets and clothing. They broke open beer and brandy barrels and drank until they were drunk. Liquid courage set in which lead to more destruction. The colonists crowded in their pathetic rundown fort for safety.

When the Peach War, as this conflict has come to be known, was at its peak, Governor Stuyvesant returned from his victory in Delaware to find his village badly damaged. In the three-day war, the Indians killed about one hundred colonists, took 150 captives, and destroyed twenty-eight farms. In New Amsterdam, five hundred head of cattle died or strayed and eight thousand bushels of corn were burned. Other towns in the area were also demolished. The Indians lost sixty of their members.

Knowing that the young Indian girl had been murdered and that the Indians had a different concept of property rights, Stuyvesant realized that the colonists had provoked the war. He decided not to take revenge on the Indians. He negotiated a series of prisoner exchanges, made peace with the Indians, and rebuilt the damaged colony.

Stuyvesant set up new laws. No new farms could be established in unprotected sections of land. Indians were not allowed to stay overnight in the city or enter it carrying weapons. Anyone caught selling Indians liquor would be punished bodily. Any Indian found drunk would be put in jail until he confessed who gave him the liquor.

"Peg-leg's" strict laws worked. Manhattan never had another war with the Indians.

The East Hampton
Witchcraft Trial
· 1658 ·

In the annals of witch trials, Salem, Massachusetts, comes to mind first and foremost. But in New York, in the town of East Hampton, people were accused of being witches for the slightest odd behaviors. Unlike most of the Salem trials, sometimes in East Hampton the "witch" came out the winner.

Elizabeth Blanchard Garlick faced trial, according to the court records, for "some detestable and wicked Arts, commonly called Witchcraft and Sorcery, did (as is suspected) maliciously and feloniously, practice at the said town of Seatalcott in the East Riding of Yorkshire on Long Island."

It started one day when Goody (short for Goodwife) Bishop went to visit the house of a sick woman named Goody Simon with some dockweed, a healing herb that she obtained from Goody Garlick. The herbs were supposed to stop Goody Simon's fits. While taking the herbs, Goody Simon noticed a black thing enter her house. Goody Simon identified the black thing as a cat and said it belonged to Goody Garlick. In those days, it was "known" that witches turned themselves into animals or spirits to do their evil deeds. Goody Simon "recoiled in horror and threw the herbs in the fire" when she found out the herbs were from Goody Garlick. As Goody Simon threw the herbs into the fire, she yelled that she did not want Goody Garlick near her or in her house because she practiced witchcraft. These accusations were brought before the magistrate at a time when the concerns of women were normally not taken seriously.

Young women often accused older women of witchcraft. Goody Garlick was in her mid-fifties when she went to visit Goody Davis. During the visit, Goody Garlick complimented Goody Davis on how pretty her baby looked. She then said, "The child is not well, for it groaneth." Upon hearing these words, Goody Davis, who had already been widowed twice and had experienced her fair share of misfortunes in life, grew very anxious. It was said that she saw death on the child's face.

The baby immediately became sick and died five days later. During the short illness, the child never opened its eyes or cried. Goody Davis made the incredible claim—which she would later repeat in court testimony—that Goody Garlick killed her baby with the "evil eye." It was Goody Davis's belief that the envy of an older woman, beyond her child-bearing years, turned Goody Garlick's fond gaze into one of jealous hostility. While Goody Garlick was merely making an observation, Goody Davis took it as some sort of threat. At the time, infant mortality rates were high, causing nervousness among all new mothers.

With two accusations of witchcraft already against her, Goody Garlick was due for her third, which happened shortly after. Arthur Howell came home one February evening to find his sixteen-year-old wife Elizabeth Howell curled up by the fireplace. Elizabeth commented "Love, I am very ill of my head, and I fear I shall have the fever." As she was placed into her bed, nursing her baby by her side, she remarked, "Lord have mercy upon us."

Since she was ill, her husband took the child from her, and she immediately became petrified and started screaming. "A witch! A witch! Now you come to torture me because I spoke two or three words against you!" At this point her father, Lion Gardiner, came running into the room to see what his daughter was yelling about. He saw his daughter just staring at the foot of her bed and sobbing that she saw "a black thing at the bed's feet." Finally exhausted, she drifted to sleep.

By the next morning her condition had made a turn for the worse. She confided in her mother, Mary Gardiner, "Oh, mother, am bewitched . . . I am not dreaming, I am not asleep. Truly I am bewitched." Her mother asked, "Whom do you see?" Elizabeth replied "Goody Garlick! Goody Garlick in the further corner and a black thing at the hither corner, both at the feet of the bed." She turned to Goody Simon, who was also present at the time, and declared that Goody Garlick "is a double-tongued woman. Did you not see her last night stand by the bedside ready to pull me in pieces? And she pricked me with pins." Elizabeth kept ranting and raving until she slipped into the arms of death.

Goody Garlick was nowhere near the scene at the time of Elizabeth's death. Yet the magistrate had to take these charges seriously. Not being skilled in the area of demonology, he decided to hand the case over to the Connecticut Court, which had experience with the Occult Doctrine. The Connecticut Court had tried eight cases of witchcraft since 1647. All accused were sentenced to hanging; two fled and escaped.

In May of 1658, the court indicted Goody Garlick with the following crime:

> Elizabeth Garlick, thou art indicted by the name of Elizabeth Garlick the wife of Joshua Garlick of East Hampton, that not having the fear of God before thine eyes thou hast entertained Satan, the Great Enemy of God and Mankind, and by his help since the year 1650 hath done works above the course of nature to the loss of lives of several persons (with several other sorceries), and in particular the wife of Arthur Howell . . . for which, according to the laws of God and the established law of this Commonwealth, thou deservest to die.

Connecticut law called for the death penalty. Before she could be sentenced, the court had to have sufficient evidence to prove that Goody Garlick somehow had cast a painful spell on Elizabeth Howell without being present the night of her death. Evidence could be obtained either through a voluntary confession or through "witchmarks," which were distinctive marks on the body of the witch herself. These "witchmarks" were said to be caused by either evil spirits or the Devil himself, sucking on a discretely located part of the witch's body. While Goody Garlick was in the jail cell during the trial, guards were posted outside her door to make sure these spirits didn't sneak into her cell to feed.

During three weeks of hearings, thirteen depositions were taken, most of which contained hearsay testimony. Goody Davis, the chief accuser, did not testify herself but gave statements to the magistrates through others. She blamed Goody Garlick not only for the death of her child but for other personal misfortunes. Richard Stratton's deposition was based on the word of Goody Davis. He testified that Goody Davis "did not know of anyone on the island who could do it unless it were Goody Garlick." All the witnesses to the mysterious death of Elizabeth Howell testified, except her father, Lion Gardiner, who was the most powerful and prominent man in East Hampton. There is not one record that can be found of his speaking a word before the court as to what his opinions were at the time. His silence on the matter is said to have helped Goody Garlick. There is also no record of a confession from Goody Garlick and no records that witch's marks were found on her body.

Goody Garlick was found not guilty, "having . . . passed a legall tryall therevpon; wherevpon, tho there did not appear sufficient Evidence to proue her guilty, yet we cannot but well approue and commend the Christian Care and Prudence of those in Authority with you, in searching into yt [sic] Case." There was not enough evidence to convict her, but they didn't acquit her either. Her husband, Joshua Garlick, had to post a bond to make sure his wife would be on her best behavior.

Goody Garlick was one of the lucky "witches." She escaped sure death. It was believed that although the court thought the suspicions were just, they chose not to anger the Devil by killing one of his "own" when they couldn't prove her guilt or innocence beyond a shadow of a doubt.

Elizabeth Garlick and her husband Joshua continued to live in East Hampton. Mysteriously, Goody Garlick's date of death is nowhere to be found.

The Notorious Captain Kidd
· 1696 ·

Terrible were the tales told of Captain Kidd, the greatest pirate ever to sail from New York City—Tales of ransom letters written in the blood of women and children he kidnapped and murdered, legends of climbing onto honest men's ships with evil in his blackened heart in a quest for gold and jewels, and stories of buried treasures found in Gardner's Island at the end of Long Island—but they weren't necessarily true.

In 1696, Captain William Kidd, a successful shipmaster, at the request of the governor of New York, was given two commissions from the King of England addressed to "our trusty and well-beloved Captain Kidd." One commission was to suppress the ravages of piracy and save commercial ships from these unmerciful mongrels. The Navy was too weak and low on manpower to patrol the seas, so brave, bold men had to be brought in to protect the innocent merchants. The second commission was to cruise as a privateer against the French. The only drawback to being a privateer was there was no pay under contract unless pirate ships were taken. No pay, no food. His life depended on it.

Captain Kidd's secret desire was to become captain of the King's Royal Navy warships, not a pirate hunter. He had been approached once prior for this purpose by the powerful Whig political party, at the time in charge of the trade commission, but he had declined. His options were narrowing. He realized he would never be captain, so he sailed to England, agreed to become a pirate hunter, and aligned himself with the powerful men of the day, the Whigs.

One February morning in 1696, heading for the pirate-filled waters of Madagascar, Malabar, and the Red Sea region in his ship the *Adventure Galley*, with its thirty-four powerful guns and crew of seasoned men, a boastful Captain Kidd failed to give a mariner's salute to the royal yachts as he left the dock. Instead, his crew members "Clapped their backsides in unison," thus insulting the lordships. Shortly after, a small boat arrived with orders from the king to take one hundred of Kidd's best men away from him as punishment. Kidd tried to recruit other men while in England, but the navy had taken all the available men. Kidd sailed back to New York to look for more sailors. His little prank had backfired.

In New York, he ran into the same problem. He had to take men from jail to make up the rest of his crew—beggars and thieves who gratefully were willing to go on the ship and sign a contract on a "no prey—no pay" basis. Some of these unsavory men knew about ships and sailing, but most of them were inexperienced. Kidd had to make the best of it. On September 6, 1696, he kissed his wife and daughters goodbye, left his house on Pearl Street, and set sail with 152 men to capture pirates and fulfill his commission.

But he could not find any pirates. Meanwhile, his ship sprung a leak and daily the men had to pump water out of the ship to keep the water level down. The food was rotting, they were short on supplies, and tempers were high. The lot of unruly ex-cons was getting anxious. Tropical temperatures were taking their toll on the men, and parasites, scurvy, and other diseases were weakening them. Many died, and the skull and crossbones flag signaling a death onboard flew constantly.

On December 12, 1696, they finally spotted a likely prey and prepared to open fire. As they got closer, they realized it was an English ship; Captain Kidd refused to attack. One of his shipmates, a gunner named William Moore, wanted to take the ship anyway. This was the beginning of the mutiny. As time went on, Kidd's men started turning against him. They had no money, no food, and no relief was in sight.

Desperate, the *Adventure Galley* docked at a place called Matta for water and food. One of the natives of Matta killed one of Kidd's sailors. The crew, already hot-tempered, stormed the island and set fire to a house. They took native hostages. Word of Captain Kidd's violent men spread, and the first legends of piracy started to surround his ship.

The ship lurked at sea, waiting for prizes to capture. Finally, they came upon a ship flying a French flag. They opened fire. As cannon balls were being hurled at the ship, the French flag came down and the English flag, the Union Jack, went up. They had fired at their own men on the ship *Maiden*. Word of this spread, and the story of the burning of the house grew to a story of Kidd's men burning a whole town. They were now labeled as pirates.

So far, Kidd had not actually committed piracy. But shortly after entering the Malabar Coast, a trader ship from Bombay flying English colors came into sight. Without orders, the men fired a shot across its bow and quickly overtook the ship. The captain, Thomas Parker, came aboard Kidd's ship. While Captain Kidd and Captain Parker were talking, Kidd's restless men climbed aboard Parker's ship and, to amuse themselves, seized Parker's men, tied their wrists behind their backs, and violently lifted their bodies with ropes, pulling their arms out of the shoulder sockets. They beat others, trying to get them to reveal secrets of hidden treasure on board. With this act, Kidd and his men were now the pirates they were accused of being.

Captain Kidd was now having trouble docking and getting supplies, as people thought he would ravage their town. Kidd felt he was only trying to carry out his commission.

Desperate, Kidd tried to gain control of the situation onboard the ship, this time using punishment as his weapon. Kidd tried to cover up the act of piracy and keep himself in the favor of the king.

But the men knew this was not possible. Finally, the heat, lack of supplies, illness, and frustration at Kidd not allowing ships to be destroyed, made them turn to gunnner William Moore to challenge Kidd's authority. Kidd called Moore a "lousie dog" for challenging him, picked up a wooden bucket, and smashed him on the head. Moore died the next day of a fractured skull. Kidd was now considered a murderer.

A break came when Kidd and his men finally captured a French ship, the *November*, and took the French passes to prove that they were following the orders of Kidd's commission and not committing piracy. Members of the *November*'s crew were bought aboard Kidd's ship as slaves. Kidd was acting legally in capturing a French ship and splitting the spoils among the men. But the ship had little wealth, so a month later Kidd seized another French ship just to gain supplies.

Vast treasures came from his capture of the *Quedah Merchant*. Bags of gold and silver, chests of jewels, and many fine silk clothes became his booty. At this point, Kidd became the target of an all-out manhunt. He was wanted for piracy for his capture of the *Maiden* as well as the *Quedah Merchant*, since the latter was taken after England had signed a peace treaty with France.

Desperate to clear his name, Kidd sailed to New York and hid out so he could negotiate with Richard Coote, the Earl of Bellomont, vice-admiral, and a Whig member of Parliament. Bellomont was one of Kidd's original sponsors. Kidd wanted

Bellomont to explain to his accusers that he was only acting according to his commission.

To secure himself in the future, Kidd buried some of his treasure between Gardner's Island and Block Island. He is said to have killed his Mastiff dog and buried it on top of the treasure, so anyone coming upon it would think it was just the grave of a dog. Some legends state Kidd also killed other pirates to protect his treasures from plunder.

Kidd wanted to make sure that his wife was safe also. He brought her aboard his ship and sailed up the Hudson to keep her away from his enemies. He left her in the care of a Negro woman who lived at the bottom of Kaaterskill Clove in Green County. Then he left and went back to the city. With wife and treasure secured, it was time to negotiate.

But his wife was not safe for long. Kidd's enemies captured her and brought her to a house in Leeds, New York. They tortured her and finally killed her by dragging her behind a white horse with a rope tied around her neck. Shortly after she was buried, some said her ghost could be seen being dragged by the galloping horse. Kidd was unaware of his wife's fate.

As Kidd's notoriety increased and tales of his treasure worth 400,000 pounds sterling grew, the hunt for Kidd increased. Kidd contacted Bellomont through friends. Bellomont, who was in need of money, at this point was deciding whether or not he should capture Kidd as his king's papers commanded and get a third of any loot seized. But by doing so he would be in direct violation of a contract with his sponsors in New York and the Whig lords who were still very powerful. Bellomont wrote a convincing letter to Kidd assuring him of his safety if he came out of hiding.

Captain Kidd came out of hiding to face his accusers. Bellomont decided to turn against Kidd and have him arrested.

As Captain Kidd sat in a small stone prison in Boston, Bellomont desperately searched for his treasure. It would have been better for Kidd to have been swallowed by the sea than endure the horrible political fate that awaited him. Captain Kidd became a pawn. Rumors were spread to build up his thievery legends. In 1701, two years after he was caught and accused of murder and piracy, and after having been treated horribly in jail, he remained isolated from the outside world with no chance of communicating with anyone who could help him. He then came before six judges at the Old Bailey Court in England where he was found guilty and given two death sentences. His documents, the French passes he took from the November and the Quedah Merchant to prove he was acting on his commission's orders, were denied him.

He was hanged on May 23, 1701 and his body was suspended in an iron cage by the Thames River to rot as a lesson to others against piracy.

Some of Captain Kidd's treasures were recovered from Gardner's Island in 1699. Some say chests of gold still lie beneath the pedestal of the Statue of Liberty on Liberty Island. People have attempted to recover these treasures, but no one to date has been successful. Ghosts of Captain Kidd and the pirates he supposedly killed to guard the treasure are said to have chased them away.

The Trial of
Peter Zenger
· 1735 ·

When John Peter Zenger arrived in New York from Germany in 1710 to work as an apprentice at the *New York Gazette*, he had no clue that he would change the course of American journalism by helping to establish the very principles on which truth can be used as a complete defense against libel.

In 1733, New York Colonial Governor William Cosby was causing a lot of controversy with his incompetence and unethical activities. He was in power, and he would stop anybody in his way to keep control. Governor Cosby arbitrarily prosecuted the interim governor, Rip Van Dam, and had Chief Justice Lewis Morris removed from the courts. This did not sit well with these wealthy and powerful men.

At the time, the only newspaper in New York City was the government-controlled *New York Gazette*. If the government didn't like what was written, it wasn't printed. So former Chief Justice Morris and the brilliant lawyer and journalist James Alexander joined forces and convinced Zenger to use his own print shop, which he had established in 1725, to publish an opposition paper called the *New York Weekly Journal*. On November 5, 1733, the first issue came out, with Zenger as publisher and editor. All contributors were anonymous.

The *New York Weekly Journal* printed articles and satirical cartoons about the governor's misconduct. James Alexander wrote many of the articles with the full approval of Zenger, who could barely speak English but was a courageous printer and patriot who knew what he believed in.

Week after week, these articles and cartoons infuriated Governor Cosby. He tried desperately to get a grand jury indictment against the printer but was unable to. Finally, using his own power, he had an executive council arrest Zenger on November 17, 1735, with the charge of "seditious libel." To twist the knife even further, Governor Cosby had the bail set so high that no one could come to his rescue, and Zenger had to sit in the dark, dreary jail cell for nine months while waiting for his trial date. But this still didn't stop the paper from being printed. Through the keyhole of his jail cell, Zenger was allowed to speak to his wife and servants, and they continued to print the paper.

In a further effort to squash Zenger and ensure his conviction, Governor Cosby appointed his own chief justice and associates to preside over Zenger's case. James Alexander questioned the ethics of this and was disbarred.

Despite illegal attempts by the governor's faction to fix the jury, a suitable "one was finally selected and the trial began on August 4, 1735. Even still, the governor was very confident because by law, the definition of libel was "any printed attack upon a public official"—which Zenger had done.

Governor Cosby, the attorney general, and the chief justice, however, were thrown completely off-guard when out of the crowd of spectators stepped a distinguished attorney from Philadelphia named Andrew Hamilton to take over as counsel for the defense. Hamilton attacked the case from a completely different angle. He admitted right up front that the *Weekly Journal* had indeed printed "alleged libels" (articles that could be interpreted as offensive to the governor), but that the information was true and therefore not libelous. He argued that in the spirit of freedom, the paper had a right to print matters that were "supported with truth."

This was an unheard-of approach. The truth as a defense against a charge of criminal libel had not been used before in either the United States or Britain. But Hamilton went for it anyway.

> For though I freely acknowledge that there are such things as libels, yet I must insist, at the same time, that what my client is charged with is not libel. And I observed just now that Mr. Attorney [Richard Bradley], in defining a libel, made use of the words "scandalous, seditious, and tend to disquiet the people." But (whether with design or not I will not say) he omitted the word "false."

Richard Bradley denied omitting the word "false," but said it did not matter anyway, since "it has been said already that it may be a libel, notwithstanding it may be true." Hamilton wouldn't let it rest.

> I still must differ with Mr. Attorney, for I depend upon it, we are to be tried upon this information now before the court and jury, and to which we have pleaded guilty, and by it we are charged with printing and publishing a certain false, malicious, seditious and scandalous libel. This word 'false' must have some meaning, or else how came it there?

Hamilton's argument posed all kinds of problems for the chief justice. If the court accepted this as a defense, a public review of all the governor's activities would have to be examined to see if the paper was printing articles based on the truth about the corruption in the Cosby administration.

The court dismissed this argument stating, "You cannot be admitted, Mr. Hamilton, to give the truth of a libel in evidence. A libel is not to be justified; for it is nevertheless a libel." Then the chief justice sternly instructed the jury to decide the case only on the fact of whether the paper printed articles and cartoons which could be construed as libel. The court would then determine the law on what the definition of libel was.

Hamilton had no recourse other than to courageously override the explicit instructions of the judge to the jury and tell them that it was indeed their right and duty to "determine both the law and the fact." They had the power as a jury of his peers to determine whether there were "falsehoods in Zenger's papers."

In his moving and eloquent closing argument, Hamilton appealed to the jury's sense of duty to fellow countrymen.

> Gentlemen of the jury, it is to you we must now appeal, for witness, to the truth of the facts we have offered, and are denied the liberty to prove. . . . The law supposes you to be summoned out of the neighborhood where the fact [crime] is alleged to committed, and the reason of your being taken out of the neighborhood is because you are supposed to have the best knowledge of the fact that is to be tried. . . . you are citizens of New York; you are really what the law supposes you to be, honest and lawful men. . . . As we have been denied the liberty of giving evidence to prove the truth of what we have published, . . . [bear in mind] that the suppressing of evidence ought always to be taken for the strongest evidence.

There is heresy in law as well as in religion . . . . it is not two centuries ago that a man would have been burned as a heretic for owning such opinions in matters of religions are publicly written and printed at this day.

Hamilton went on to ask if we can speak freely about our God, then why can't we speak our minds about our government if it is true? "Were this to be denied, then the next step may make them slaves."

Hamilton brilliantly pointed out examples in the Bible, from jokes, and many situations where innuendoes could be construed as libel. Libel, he said, is a way for people in power to suppress opposition and hide behind the law.

Then Hamilton appealed to the jury's sense of freedom. "The loss of liberty to a generous mind is worse than death. . . . Men who injure and oppress the people under their administration provoke them to cry out and complain." In a final passionate burst, he then implored the jury to deliver an uncorrupt verdict by "both exposing and opposing arbitrary power (in these parts of the world, at least) by speaking and writing the truth."

As the front page of the *New York Weekly Journal* of August 18, 1735 read, "The jury returned in Ten Minutes, and found me Not Guilty."

Peter Zenger's trial was a landmark victory establishing freedom of the press, truth as a defense against libel, and the right of a jury to consider the law as well as the facts of a publication of supposed libel. The courage of Zenger, Hamilton, and Alexander changed the course of history forever and gave Americans the freedom to speak their minds.

Note: You can visit the John Peter Zenger Memorial Room in New York City in the Federal Hall Memorial Museum on Pine Street in Manhattan.

The Battle of Brooklyn

· 1776 ·

In 1775, members of the mighty British army were surprised when they were unexpectedly attacked at Lexington and Concord and then defeated at Breeds Hill in Massachusetts. With its pride hurt, the British government vowed revenge, and America and England became locked into mortal conflict.

In the late eighteenth century, the common man in the American colonies still looked to the English king for protection. The colonists refused to be ruled by Parliament, which was run by feudal lords and filled with corruption. So, naturally, the American colonists turned to King George III to intercede on their behalf when Parliament infringed on the freedom they wanted.

But King George had other plans. He told Parliament that he wanted the American rebellion crushed, and he was willing to pull out all the stops and use the full force of the British army to do it. He was even willing to hire German mercenaries, just to make sure the job was done right.

In March of 1776, the stage was set. George Washington was appointed the commander in chief of the Continental army. He was the rebels' hope for victory. Joining his ranks were leftovers from Benedict Arnold's army—regiments from Pennsylvania, Maryland, and Virginia. In total, Washington commanded about twenty thousand soldiers.

Washington had the men build a fort, later named Fort Washington, on the northern end of Manhattan Island. He had two of his men, Nathaniel Greene and Rufus Putnam, survey the land and build up its defenses. They got Henry Knox to build the battery—a line of cannons aimed out into New York Harbor to defend against incoming enemy ships.

Washington strategically had his troops spread out on both sides of the East River and all along Manhattan Island. But no matter how great a general he was, Washington was at a disadvantage. He had no navy at his disposal to protect the waters in New York Harbor. To make matters worse, he had troops that were undisciplined and had little respect for the military. He had a shortage of heavy artillery, and even if he'd had the artillery, his men had no experience using the weapons. The odds were absolutely against him. His only option was to threaten, "If any man turns his back . . . I will shoot him through."

Enter the enemy on June 29, 1776, just prior to the signing of the Declaration of Independence. Playing the lead role in the British army and entering from across the Atlantic Ocean was General William Howe, accompanied by a powerful force of thirty-two thousand men, nine thousand of them German mercenaries.

It looked as if all of London had come to invade the American shores. It was the largest British force to come to America to date and all of the soldiers were there with one goal—to destroy

Washington and his men and keep America from gaining independence from England. Seeing the German mercenaries with the British regiments was a wake-up call to the Colonists. America and England were now in a state of war.

The British forces sailed eighty-eight frigates into Graves End, Staten Island, without resistance from the Americans. Why? The battery of cannons that Henry Knox built was facing the wrong way! It was useless as a defense against the British onslaught.

But the wind gods were in Washington's favor. Strong gusts prevented Howe from sailing warships up the East River. Washington seized the moment and rowed men back and forth across the river until he built up reinforcements on the Brooklyn side. For three days the winds blew and Howe's ships were stuck, giving Washington the time he needed to reposition his ill-equipped men. Washington split his army in two, half in Brooklyn with their backs to the East River and half in New York City with the mislaid cannons. On August 26, the winds subsided and Howe was able to sail his warships up the river. He then marched ten thousand of his men around the American positions in a flanking maneuver.

The British even stopped at the Rising Sun Tavern, had a few drinks, then forced the tavern owner to show them a passage called Rockaway Path (today's Evergreen Cemetery), so they could march down what is now Eastern Parkway to Bedford. Then, in a surprise attack, they struck the Americans behind their defensive line.

The Americans knocked down a large oak tree and fought from behind it. (Today, a marker in Prospect Park marks the spot.) Realizing that they had been ambushed, some of the American soldiers fled. They were chased into the woods and bayoneted near today's Atlantic Avenue. At this point, Washington realized he had maneuvered his army into a trap.

The British also drove forward on the western shoreline with more reinforcements. The Americans counterattacked with reinforcements from Connecticut, New York, Pennsylvania, Delaware, and Maryland. Although the Colonists were inexperienced and still badly outnumbered, they were ready to die for their country. The Brits were amazed at the determination and valor of the untrained American troops.

As the British advanced, the Americans kept falling the line back to a more fortified position. The only advantages the Americans had were their position on higher ground and a small stream in front of them that could only be crossed by a narrow bridge.

The Americans held their ground as the British troops kept moving closer. They were holding up at a place called the Stone House, surrounded on all sides by British soldiers.

Even though he had only four hundred men in his Maryland brigade, General Sterling felt there was only one way to stop the inexhaustible British—to attack. The Marylanders bravely flung themselves, with bayonets in hand, into a rain of fire from the oncoming British troops. Stunned, the British recoiled, but only for a moment. Soon, the ground was filled with dead and dying Marylanders. Sterling gathered up his remaining men and again they attacked. Six times Sterling charged, and twice the unexpected assaults drove the British away from the Stone House. Washington and other generals looked on from an observation post on a nearby hill, thinking the Marylanders would surrender. When he saw them repeatedly attack, Washington cried "Good God! What brave fellows I must this day lose!"

After the sixth attack, 256 out of barely 400 men laid dead in front of the Stone House. Their heroic fighting gave Washington and his men the time they needed to retreat and escape across Gowanus Creek and survive. Sterling himself was caught by the British. His sacrifice was remembered throughout the war, and someone once said, "The Declaration of Independence that was signed in ink in Philadelphia was signed in blood in South Brooklyn."

Then a rainstorm with the force of a "noreaster" came in.

On August 29th, Washington, with the wind in his favor

again, decided it was time to retreat from Brooklyn in a strategic move. General Howe was now basking in victory and wanted to push forward to close in on the remaining American troops. He had a clear run to the earthworks where they were hiding and decided to go for it, but the winds delayed him.

Meanwhile, Washington was exiting out the back door with his troops, knowing that if the British saw him retreating across the East River, his troops would be killed instantly. It was a chance he had to take. In complete silence, the American troops rowed themselves and their equipment across the East River from Brooklyn to Manhattan, a very difficult and daring feat to accomplish—a feat that required masterful precision and efficiency. As one British military critic put it, "this retreat should hold a high place among military transactions."

While Washington's previous misjudgments had put the American army into a perilous position, this move saved the force in the end. When the confident British army moved into Brooklyn to do the final sweep and wipe out the Americans, all they found were some rusted buckets.

With some time to regroup, Washington went on to fight many more battles in the Revolutionary War. Although many men were captured and killed while under Washington's leadership, Washington's skill as a tactician—along with his bold and daring courage to fight against the odds and keep slipping away from the enemy—eventually led him to win the war.

The Battle of Brooklyn, in terms of both troops and casualties, almost brought America to its knees. But despite the fact that the British had thirty thousand men, it did not shake the fight for freedom. It goes down in history as one of the nation's greatest battles in the fight for independence.

The Invincible
Murphy
· 1780 ·

The first travelers to Schoharie, in today's Albany County, described it as "a scene of extraordinary beauty . . . no traces of any occupants of this valley were seen, except here and there the ruins of a deserted wigwam." These travelers "returned to Albany and gave such a flattering account of the country . . . that the whole company started immediately for Schoharie."

In their rush to settle in the town, the travelers left themselves open to an attack. America was, after all, in a war with Britain. However, one man, the invincible Timothy Murphy, a distinguished native Virginian and marksman, was known as the "Benefactor of Schohaire." He had defended the village against Tories and Indians in the past and would help again now.

Murphy, well built, five feet, six inches tall, with a dark complexion and eyes full of passion, was as quick as lightning and apparently nothing short of a superman. Murphy served in many battles and his expert marksmanship earned him a place in July 1777 with the Morgan's Rifle Corps, an elite organization. So sharp was his eye, he was able to hit a seven-inch target from 250 yards away. His skill made him one of five hundred riflemen hand-picked to serve under Sir John Burgoyne during the invasion of northern New York during the Revolutionary War. His body of steel apparently could not be harmed. And although he was in many battles and wars, he was never wounded. He became known as "the terror of the Tories and Indians" after he killed many key players in the British command.

His reputation became so well known that even though he wasn't a commander, his advice was taken on attack procedures. The commanding officers themselves would defer to his judgment, since he seemed to be extremely skilled in every level of fighting. His enemies made many plans to destroy him, but he always managed to escape. He said he "loved danger for danger's sake."

One account that created his legend began with him becoming separated from the rest of his party. A slew of Indians was pursuing him. He outran them all except one. Instead of running faster, he simply turned and shot the enemy, killing him. He thought the other Indians were long gone and was taking the dead man's weapon when the rest of the Indians attacked him. He grabbed the gun of his fallen enemy from the ground and shot at the attackers. Then he turned around and discharged his own double-barrel rifle. Not knowing that he had two guns, the Indians were amazed that he was able to fire off three shots with one gun without reloading. They fled, thinking he had magical powers and that some invisible being was warding off any bullets that were aimed at him.

During the fourth year of the American Revolution, the frontier of New York was the site of the most vicious battles. The people of Schoharie were constantly bombarded with raids and attacks by the British and Indians. To defend this area, three forts were to be built, one at Upper, one at Middle, and one at Lower Schoharie Creek. But there were simply not enough men to protect the land. Timothy Murphy had returned to the Schoharie Valley to settle with his wife, Peggy, after his expiration of service in 1779. He enlisted with the 15th Regiment of the Albany County Militia and resumed patrolling the valley.

In the fall of 1780, Colonel Sir John Johnson, with eight hundred men consisting of British soldiers and Indians, decided to attack the Middle Creek fort at daybreak. Starting the attack after sunrise, the rear of his troops was discovered by the sentinels of the upper fort and an alarm gun was fired. The alarm gun was quickly answered by twenty other riflemen, led by Timothy Murphy in the middle fort. To maintain their advantage as they advanced, the British troops began burning everything in their paths: barns, houses, stacks of hay. They also killed the Americans' horses and cattle.

Murphy left the fort and positioned himself in a ditch outside the middle fort. When the advance regiments got within eighty yards of the fort, he stood up and opened fired on them. A bullet came within inches of his face, sending dirt into his eyes, but he took one more shot and brought one more Indian to the ground before he was forced to retreat back into the safety of the fort.

Inside the fort were not only men, but their wives and children as well. They too stood armed with molding bullets, loaded muskets, and spears, since the ammunition in the fort was very low.

The British attacked the fort with cannon shots that did more to frighten the commander, Major Wolsey, than cause actual damage. Wolsey was so shaken by the attacks that he hid among the women and children until his fellow soldiers embarrassed him out of hiding. Several times the fort caught fire and the women put it out. With ammunition nearly exhausted, the panicked major thought it best to surrender and ordered a white flag to be raised. Murphy disagreed with this command, knowing that surrender would mean death or long imprisonment for the people at the fort.

The officers of the militia defied Wolsey and refused to surrender. The enemy, not realizing the dwindling strength of the Americans and sensing that their own fire was having little or no effect, began preparing for another attack. When the white enemy flag demanding the fort's surrender approached, Murphy and Colonel Bartholomew Vroman suspected the enemy of trying to learn the actual strength of the garrison. They fired upon the flag and the British soldiers retreated.

Major Wolsey ordered some of the American soldiers to arrest Murphy for defying his orders, but Murphy was so popular among the troops that the order was not obeyed. The enemy's white flag approached a second time and was fired at again. When the flag approached for a third time and Murphy again prepared to shoot at it, Major Wolsey threatened to shoot him. Murphy just laughed at Wolsey's attempt at a threat. In a battle of egos, Major Wolsey ordered a white flag to be raised over the fort to signal a surrender. Murphy raised his rifle at Wolsey and stated, "I will die before they shall have me a prisoner." He then added that anyone who raised the flag would be met with instant death. With that statement, the defeated Wolsey, tail between his legs, retreated to his room. Later he was found by Colonel Vroman, trembling like a leaf in his bed with the sheets pulled over his head. A leader of the fort militia saw Wolsey's unstable state and demanded he turn over the command of the fort to him. Wolsey agreed.

Murphy and the men held tight to the fort, and Colonel Johnson, in midday, decided to continue past the fort and down into the valley, burning valuable wheat and livestock along the way. When Johnson and his men reached the lower fort, they found the people there were also well prepared, so Johnson continued past the fort into Canada, ravaging the land along the way. In the end, Johnson and his men destroyed eighty thousand bushels of grain.

But the damage could have been much worse had Murphy and his men not have held their ground and protected the middle fort. Rather than being driven out of the valley, they held Schoharie for America.

The day was won because of the bravery of the invincible Timothy Murphy.

The Doctor's Riot
· 1788 ·

A small boy ran mortified and panicked after recognizing his mother's body lined up with other corpses at the local medical school and hospital. Panting, he ran to his father, a mason, who was working near the hospital. Infuriated at what the boy told him, he dropped his tools and gathered his fellow workers to go to the hospital. Apparently, medical school employees had been digging up bodies from the local cemetery. A crowd of angry people gathered as word spread of the horrible act. By the time the man and his son arrived at New York Hospital, a crowd of five thousand people had gathered outside.

They stormed the medical college and shattered the instruments they thought had been used for dissecting the stolen bodies. They were determined to make the grave robbers pay. The mob removed all the bodies they found and reburied them, giving them a respectable resting place at last.

Rioting was commonplace in 1788. The influence of the British traditions that shaped the American colonies during the late eighteenth century sanctioned rioting. It was part of the culture. Many believed that an occasional riot was the best way to maintain a free government, so riots had widespread community support.

All the people in the street at the time of a riot were considered rioters and equally culpable according to the law. In general, the government would make only moderate attempts to stop riots as long as the rioters did not threaten too much violence or challenge the law directly. But tolerance for the disorderly conduct was coming to an end. The government was starting to use more force to squelch riots. There were four great riots towards the end of the eighteenth century. The Doctor's Riot was one in which the government wasn't sure which side to support.

Doctors had long been grave robbing to get corpses for dissection. This went against the moral fiber of the community, which strongly believed that a proper burial and an undisturbed grave were essential for a soul to go to heaven. People believed that if a grave was disturbed, the ghost of the deceased would remain on this earth and haunt family and friends. Therefore, it was very important for the bodies of loved ones to remain where they were laid. Anyone who did anything to disturb their eternal peace was subject to the wrath of those still living.

When the crowd stormed the hospital on that thirteenth day of April in 1788, they were on a mission. They were not there to damage the building. They were there to right the wrongs that the doctors and medical students had inflicted on the dead. After capturing and abusing the doctors and medical students, the rioters turned them over to the authorities only after it was agreed that there would be legal action taken against them for their horrendous thievery. The government was sympathetic to the cries of the people and their moral outrage. They kept the students and doctors in jail for their own "safe keeping," and to pacify the crowd.

The following morning the crowd was still angry and a new riot broke out. The authorities still did not want to use force and were waiting to see if the atmosphere would calm down. But the mob turned ugly and more violent. They weren't satisfied with the guilty being held in jail cells. They wanted revenge. The mob demanded that they be allowed to reexamine the medical school. They wanted to make sure they had taken all the bodies and treated them properly. Hoping again to calm the rioters, the governor, mayor, and other government officials allowed them to search the school buildings again. But the masses pushed further. Next they wanted to search the doctors' houses for stolen bodies. The authorities agreed again, as long as they were allowed to come along to protect the property and homes of the physicians and make sure the search was done in an orderly fashion. For the moment, the crowd was satisfied.

The mayhem, however, continued during the afternoon when the crowd became intent on attacking the arrested medical students in jail. Authorities refused to surrender the prisoners to the angry attackers. The tension rose. Fearful magistrates called upon the militia, hoping to get the situation under control. But the mob surrounded one patrol, seizing and breaking its weapons. Later, the rest of the militia came under attack, and Governor Clinton, General von Steuben, John Jay, and other prominent citizens were assaulted for defending the doctors at the jail.

With rocks and brickbats raining down on them, the officials ordered the militia to open fire. Three rioters were killed—a cartman, a young man, and a person identified only as a "servant of Mr. Livingston's."

The next day, the police and government officials called in a larger militia, fearing another outburst. This time, the mob, seeing the large number of troops, decided to keep order, remain calm, and end the riot. Only three people were arrested for their part in the uprising.

Newspaper accounts of the riots condemned both the doctors and the rioters. The *New York Journal* used half of its coverage to denounce the actions of the medical community. "It is no wonder the spirit of the citizens is aroused," they said, "it is not only the vulgar, but all ranks [who] join in condemning these scandalous enormities. . . . There is little doubt, but this specimen of the public sentiment will fully check the practices of stealing the dead."

Even the judge, Chief Justice Richard Morris, at the trial of the three arrested rioters, had mixed sentiments about the riots when he spoke to the grand jury. "Though it [the riot] may be palliated in the first stages of it . . . after every search was made to satisfy the wishes of the people, the attack upon the jail, and the insults to the Magistrates were altogether inexcusable."

The rioters believed the doctors went too far in reaching into the graves in the name of research. The whole incident could have been avoided had they just let the dead rest in peace.

Burning of the Steamship Phoenix
·1819·

Nearly one hundred years before the disaster of the *Titanic*, a similar tragedy occurred in Lake Champlain. "A burning vessel, in the dead of night, and three miles from the nearest land" blazed brightly as the passengers onboard awakened and scrambled to save their lives.

As the passengers onboard the steamer *Phoenix* stepped out of their cabin doors, they were met with blinding flames that gave them little hope of survival. So intense and encompassing were the flames that one passenger recounted that, "the thought struck me that no other way of escape was left but to plunge half naked through the blaze into the water."

The steamer was so illuminated by the flames in the middle of the night that it appeared to be as bright at the midday sun. "I fancied it was the torch of death, to point me and my fellow-travelers to the tomb," the same passenger recalled. Desperate, many ran to the gangplanks to try to get on the lifeboats and attempted to cut the rope holding the boats before the boats were filled to capacity. Some passengers, confident of their swimming skills, grabbed a plank of sufficient buoyancy and jumped into the water.

The night was gloomy and ominous and the wind was directly ahead of the ship, forcing the fire back into the boat with such force that as it came down the middle of the ship, it threatened to instantly destroy everything in its path.

The only place of refuge appeared to be the bow, as the wind was not aimed in that direction. But the flames, like those that blocked the Roman chariots in Exodus, were an insurmountable wall, forcing those aboard to stay by the stern.

At this early hour, the temporary commander of the ship, the twenty two year old son of Captain Richard M. Sherman, acted with promptness and energy. He remained calm, cool, and collected.

Methodically, in the midst of mass hysteria, as the passengers were rushing about to seize the lifeboats and dispatch them half-full, young Sherman thought only of saving *all* the passengers. Taking charge of the situation, he boldly stood in the gangway with a pistol in each hand to prevent any person from releasing the lifeboats before they were filled.

Young Sherman wanted to assure that all the women and children were on the lifeboats before he lowered them. When he was about to release the boats, he discovered a Mrs. Wilson who had, in a petrified state, walked out of her cabin, looked at the flames and simply walked back in, securing herself to a wooden bench and refusing to let go. Upon the captain's persistence and among her shrills and shrieks, he managed to pry her from the bench and escort her safely aboard a lifeboat.

Once he was assured that the boats were now filled to capacity, he had them lowered safely into the lake. The boats then traveled three miles to the nearest shore.

All the while, the steamship *Phoenix* moved forward in the water. The lifeboats returned and anchored themselves with a rope to the burning ship so passengers could board. Violent waves smashed the lifeboats into the *Phoenix*, and the terrified passengers in the lifeboats clung to the *Phoenix* for security. They would not untie the lifeboats. Young Sherman thought to cut the fast rope holding the lifeboats and they drifted away from the sinking ship.

After the second wave of passengers were safely onshore, the rowers of the lifeboats returned to the burning ship to rescue the crew and the remaining passengers. There wasn't enough room on the third load to take the young captain, so he stayed behind on the sinking inferno, secure that he was the only living soul left on the ship.

As he watched the lifeboats drift into the darkness for the third time, he took one last look around the ship and discovered the *Phoenix's* chambermaid under a settee. She was unconscious. Young Sherman tied her to a plank that he had secured for his own escape and placed her in the water, pushing her towards the safety of the shore.

He was now totally alone on the ship. Feeling confident and satisfied that he had saved the lives of all the people entrusted to him, he leapt from the burning wreck, just before the lake swallowed the demolished ship. Using the settee as a floatation device he reached the shore safely.

Later, reporting on these extraordinary acts of heroism, one of the *Phoenix's* passengers wrote,

> Amid the confusion, danger, and difficulties attendant on this terrible disaster, he displayed an energy and presence of mind, not only worthy of the highest praise, but which we might seek for in vain, even among those in riper years. To qualities like these, rightly directed as they were, was it owing that *not a person was lost* on that fearful night.

In 1840, young Captain Sherman commanded another boat on Lake Champlain and became known to all who traveled his route as Captain Sherman of the steamboat *Burlington.*

His courageous actions that night are among the most heroic ever displayed by a boating captain. Had the *Titanic* had such a brave captain, maybe more lives would have been saved.

First New York Locomotive Throws Passengers Around
·1831·

Curiosity seekers and thousands of spectators jammed every possible position along the tracks from Pinkster Hill in Albany to Schenectady to witness the first train, the DeWitt Clinton, named after the governor who had created the Erie Canal, make its first journey along the seventeen-mile track. Schenectady, at the time, was the main hub of activity—the place where farmers and producers of industrial products would drop off their goods to be conveyed to marketing towns. If this train were successful in making the trip, passengers would be able to avoid a forty-mile ride through the locks of the Erie Canal, save shipping time, and transport goods through the dead of winter when the water was frozen.

In the 1830s, railroads were operated by businessmen instead of the state, causing fierce competition to build them bigger, better, and faster, and reap the profits. Anticipation was in the air. It was the era of railroad enthusiasm, and everyone across America had "railroad fever."

The Dewitt Clinton was quite a comical sight, though it must have seemed quite impressive at the time. It was built at the West Point Foundry, at the foot of Beach Street in New York City, and upon completion, it was shipped by water to Albany. It weighed in at 6,758 and 1/2 pounds and was eleven feet, six inches in length. The locomotive was rated at ten horsepower. It was mounted on four large wagon wheels of four feet, six inches in diameter—the same wheels that were used to haul horse-drawn freight. The Dewitt Clinton consisted of five parts—the front locomotive, a flat bed, and three stagecoaches for passengers all attached by chains.

At its front, the locomotive had a large metal smokestack similar to a stovepipe. A few feet behind it, in the middle of the locomotive, was a round boiler fastened and braced to the wagon bed. The boiler was bell-shaped and looked like the tin man's head from *The Wizard of Oz*. Next, hitched to the locomotive by chains, was a wooden, square-shaped flat bed carrying two wooden barrels of water and chunks of wood to use as fuel. Attached to the flat bed were three stagecoaches to be used for carrying passengers. Each stagecoach was attached by chains to the next and had its own independent driver.

The DeWitt Clinton had no headlights, no bells, no whistles, no spark arrestors to prevent fires, and no cars. The engineer stood in the middle of the locomotive on the small platform near the boiler. He had no protection from the heat or any of the machinery. The fireman passed the chunks of wood into the furnace over this small platform. Despite all these disadvantages, the Dewitt was the first locomotive to be used on the route that later became the New York Central system, the Mohawk-Hudson line.

On that hot afternoon on the ninth day of August in 1831, each driver acted as an independent collector of tickets for the people riding on his stagecoach in this exhibition excursion. The tickets had been sold to the lucky passengers, mostly rich notables, in advance, at hotels and other places in the city.

After each driver collected his tickets, he mounted the seat of his stagecoach and signaled with a tin horn that his coach was ready for departure. When all three coaches had signaled, the Dewitt Clinton was ready to take off. And take off it did.

The Dewitt lunged forward with a tremendous jerk that shoved the passengers out of their seats backward and onto the floor. Some of them banged their heads against the top of the stagecoach they were riding in. The passengers quickly scrambled to regain their seats and hold on for dear life as the Dewitt kept lurching forward. Finally, the chains became taut and the entire train moved along nicely for a few moments. Then the locomotive had to stop abruptly to make adjustments. This time the unfortunate passengers were hurled forward like rag dolls. Then the train moved forward again, and once more the passengers were dislodged from their seats—top hats flying everywhere. The onlookers found this very amusing. That was until, of course, their horses were startled by the sound of the locomotive. The panicked horses reared up on their hind legs and bolted. They took off in a wild stampede. Now there was chaos on the roads as well as in the train.

The stampeding horses crashed into buggies, carriages, and wagons and caused them to capsize. Smash-ups crowded the roads as spectators tried to steer out of the way to avoid the oncoming horses. The onlookers standing in the road scrambled for cover in every direction. Shouts, curses, and screams filled the air as utter confusion prevailed. But the Dewitt faithfully chugged on.

At one point, the train stopped at a water-station to refill the barrels. Some quick-minded observers noticed the jolting to the passengers and put a plan into action. The stagecoaches were stretched as far apart as the connecting chains would allow, then a rail from a nearby fence was placed in between to keep the coaches apart. This was the forerunner to today's brass ring dividers. This lessened the movement of the coaches when the train started and stopped, and the jerking subsided.

But the passengers had to contend with something more dangerous than being flung across the coaches. The Dewitt burned pitch pine for fuel, and the pine burned with quick, hot flames. Sparks started to shoot out of the boiler backwards— toward the passengers. The riders on the stagecoaches shielded themselves with umbrellas, which immediately caught on fire and became blazing torches. Quickly, the flaming umbrellas were thrown overboard and ignited the clothing of bystanders at the side of the road. People were now whipping their neighbors to put out the fire. Other human torches were running wildly trying to escape the flames, but the wind only spread the fire further. Luckily, no one was badly hurt, but it did create a frenzied scene.

Despite all the excitement and turmoil, the train arrived in Schenectady amidst the loud cheers of thousands. The onlookers stood proudly, admiring the arrival of the iron horse and its soot-covered and disheveled human passengers and freight.

The black-faced passengers got out, had some refreshments and without much ado, Conductor Clark yelled out for the passengers to prepare for the return journey back to Albany. The charred-clothed group climbed back aboard their coaches and resumed their seats. This time the train, without any accidents, mass commotion, or jerking and jutting movements returned the passengers to Pinkster Hill, thus marking the way for the improved railroads of the future.

As for the Dewitt itself, it only made a few other journeys. Some repairs are documented, but eventually, on November 1, 1833, the Board of Directors authorized the superintendent to dispose of the locomotive engine.

The parts were sold for $485. The last remnant of the DeWitt surfaced in 1893 when one of the old original wheels was found lying in a junk heap at the West Albany Shop.

An exhibition in the gallery of the concourse of the Grand Central Terminal in New York City has a replica of the defunct DeWitt.

The Voices of
Seneca Falls
· 1848 ·

A crowd of three hundred women and men gathered at a small Wesleyan Methodist chapel in the village of Seneca Falls on the hot summer days of July 19 and 20, 1848. The meeting on the 19th began promptly at 10 A.M. and was exclusively for women. The meetings on the second day were open to all. The convention had been called to discuss the social, civil, and religious condition of women. It was the first women's rights convention ever held.

The women at the convention felt it was time to take action. They came together to create their own declaration of independence, which they called the Declaration of Sentiments. Their goal was to make the principles of the declaration become law. "We hold these truths to be self-evident: That all men and women are created equal" was the message that rang in the ears of the audience members who listened to hours of speeches about women's rights and the lack of them.

This meeting was the launching of a daring plan that had started eight years prior when Lucretia Mott and Elizabeth Cady Stanton met at an anti-slavery convention in London. After taking a long boat ride to London to participate in this event, they were denied a place on the floor and forced to watch from behind a curtain simply because they were women. This infuriated them. These two crusaders decided to hold their own convention to focus on how women could secure the same rights as men—the rights that American women take for granted today.

The world in which Mott and Stanton lived was a world of special privileges for men. In 1840, women did not have the right to vote, speak in public, attend college, sit on juries, sue, divorce an abusive husband, get custody of their children or own property. The only jobs open to women were as teachers, seamstresses, mill workers, or maids. Married women were not allowed to move about town or even spend money against their husband's wishes. A husband was even allowed to take all the wages that his wife or child earned and spend it on liquor instead of food, and there was nothing his wife could do about it. Legally, a woman's husband controlled her. The small convention held in Seneca Falls, New York, began a revolution. It was the beginning of a seventy-five-year relentless battle to end the oppression.

Ironically, the deck was so stacked against the women that even holding the convention required the support and permission of their husbands. As Mott and Stanton drafted an agenda for the convention, one of their major concerns was whether or not to put the right to vote in the Declaration of Sentiments. Elizabeth's husband, Henry Stanton, thought the idea of women voting was ridiculous and refused to attend the convention, since the women insisted on putting it in. James Mott accepted the idea, so, since neither woman had any experience chairing a meeting, they decided that James should chair the convention.

The attendance at the conference was considered low. But even though it was held in a small town, far away from the major cities, newspapers all over the country wrote about it—mostly negatively. But even bad press helps a cause. Many women found out about the conference and ignored the snide remarks made by many of the male reporters; within the next few years women's rights conventions were held in almost every state.

Right up front the women tried to ease the worries that some people expressed, stating that they did not want to dress like men or have men head the cradles. They just wanted equal rights.

The sentiments put to the audience in Seneca Falls were simple and straightforward—laws conflicting in any way with the true happiness of women go against nature and are not valid; laws are not valid if they prevent a woman from holding a job of her choice or place her in a lower position than men; women and men are equals—they were intended to be so by the Creator and should be recognized as such; women and men have capabilities and responsibilities and should therefore have equal rights.

At first, some women were afraid to get up and speak their minds, since they had been conditioned to keep silent in public. By the second day of the convention the passion spread and women were speaking out.

> Then the Declaration of Sentiments was read:
> It is obvious that men and women are created equal. They are blessed by the Creator with certain basic rights which no one can take away. Some of these rights are life, liberty and the opportunity to make your own decisions about your life. It is the job of governments to help people live free lives. Governments get their power from the people. If a government forgets this purpose, it is the right of those who are suffering to refuse to obey it. It is the people's duty to get rid of such a government and make a new one. Women have clearly suffered under this government, and now they need to demand their equal rights.

The women knew they had a battle ahead of them to achieve this goal.

> We know we will be criticized, but we shall do everything we can to reach our goals. We shall employ agents, circulate pamphlets, petition the state and national legislatures, and try to get the churches and the press to help us. We hope this convention will be

followed by other conventions in every part of the country. We do this day affix our signatures to this declaration.

Eleven of the resolutions of the Declaration of Sentiments were passed unanimously by the convention attendees. Only one, "Resolved, That it is the duty of the women of this country to secure to themselves their sacred right to the elective franchise," met opposition. The women's suffrage movement began.

The first women's convention made the government listen more carefully to the concerns of women, even though the New York legislature at the time made fun of the women's rights movement, stating, "Ladies have the best place and choicest tidbit at the table, they have the best seat in the cars, a lady's coat costs three times a gentleman's. . . . the gentlemen are the sufferers." Some men supported the movement, however. Frederick Douglass wrote, "We bid the women engaged in this movement our humble Godspeed."

For the next seventy years women protested whenever and wherever possible, marching with their symbol, the gold sunflower, which became the symbol for the American suffrage movement. So determined were they that the early suffragists marched outside the White House and were arrested and held as the first United States political prisoners. They held numerous parades for their cause even though they were violently attacked, spit on, and cursed at. They marched in rain and freezing weather. They wrote pamphlets, collected petitions, and sent letters to Congress.

In all, suffragists held 56 referendum campaigns, 806 campaigns for the right to vote in various states, and 19 campaigns in 19 consecutive Congresses. They made hundreds of speeches and traveled thousands of miles to win support. Many women devoted their lives to the cause and in the end, the 19th Amendment, securing for women the right to vote, was ratified on August 26, 1920.

The Cardiff Giant
· 1869 ·

On the morning of October 16, 1869, farmer William "Stub" Newell asked two of his workers to dig a well behind his farm to make it more convenient for the cattle to get water. Even though his farm was already well supplied with water, the workers picked up their shovels and started to dig. Gideon Emmons and Henry Nichols dug shovelfull after shovelfull until they struck something solid, three and a half feet underground.

At first they thought they had hit a water line. But slowly, as they unearthed the line, they realized they had uncovered a human leg—a stone leg—then a foot.

"I declare, some old Indian has been buried here!" exclaimed one of the workers. Within a few minutes they revealed a massive petrified statue—10 feet, 4 1/2 inches tall, weighing 2,990 pounds. Word spread throughout the town—the Cardiff Giant was born.

The town of Cardiff was rich in history. The "long house" of the Onondaga Iroquois Indians was there, and sixteenth-century Jesuit missionaries were known to have lived in the area. The possibility that this behemoth might be a petrified man or an ancient aboriginal statue was totally acceptable to the townsfolk.

Hundreds of people from all walks of life came to view this "Onondaga Colossus," as the statue was first named. By the afternoon of the 16th, the statue was covered with a tent and people were being charged twenty-five cents to come and gawk. Soon, people flocked from all around the world to see this great discovery, each with his own theory. Preachers thought it was the Bible come to life. They quoted from Genesis 6:4—"There were giants on the earth in those days, and also afterward, when the sons of God had relations with the daughters of men, who bore children to them." The Biblical literalists believed it was a petrified man and even suggested that the figure be buried again.

Neighboring Indians said that it was the petrified body of an Onondaga Indian prophet who had flourished many centuries ago and had promised to return to the earth to see his descendants.

Scientists, paleontologists, and scholars, however, thought otherwise. Scholar Andrew White of Cornell University was an eyewitness and described the scene this way:

> Entering, we saw a large pit or grave, and, at the bottom of it, perhaps five feet below the surface an enormous fixture, apparently of Onondaga gray limestone. It was a stone giant with massive features the whole body nude, limbs contracted as if in agony. It had a color as if it had lain long in the earth, and over its surface were minute punctures, like pores. . . . Lying in its grave, with the subdued light from the roof of the tent falling upon it, and with the limbs contorted as if in a death struggle, it produced a most weird effect. An air of great solemnity pervaded the place. Visitors hardly spoke above a whisper.

His verdict—hoax. He was right.

George Hull was a Binghamton, New York cigar manufacturer and an atheist. While visiting his sister in Ackley, Iowa, he had a heated debate with a Reverend Mr. Turk about the literal interpretation in the Bible of there being giants on the earth. Angered that this reverend would blindly believe in anything, he started to devise an elaborate hoax to embarrass the reverend and make a fool out of him.

Hull purchased an acre of land in Fort Dodge, Iowa called "Gypsum Hollow." Then he quarried a five-ton block of blue-veined gypsum, because he felt these veins would give the statue he planned to build a real effect. To keep his hoax a secret, he told any nosy neighbors that he was building a stone statue as a gift from Iowa to the memorial of Abe Lincoln in Washington, DC. They bought the story.

He then transported the huge block of gypsum by wagon to a nearby train station to transport to Chicago, Illinois to the marble cutter, Edward Burghardt and his associates. The only problem was the stone was so heavy that the wagon collapsed. Having no other choice, he cut a one and a half ton section away from the block and had it sent.

Hull was very vague as to the reasons but told the sculptors that he needed his statue to be mistaken as a fossil or some type of ancient statue for his plan to work.

The cutters began to work on the shortened chunk. They sculpted a statue of a petrified giant. The giant's arm was reaching across his abdomen. His legs were twisted as if he suffered a painful death and breathed his last breath in agony. To age the surface, sulfuric acid was used. The face of the statue was modeled after Hull himself as the ultimate joke. Seventeen days later, the final touch to the statue was made to bring it to life. Darning needles were driven into the "skin" to make it look like the statue had human pores. Hull was very pleased with the creation.

With part one of his hoax set, Hull set the stage for part two. He made plans to ship the giant to his partner in crime, his relative William Newell, in upstate New York. They had to be very careful how they sent this large statue so that no one would get suspicious seeing a large box being brought to Newell's farm. An elaborate crisscrossing route was set up through backcountry and farmland. Newell's family was conveniently sent away on a mini-excursion during the time of the statue's arrival, so they would not witness anything. Whenever Hull was stopped by curious travelers he just said the box contained a tobacco-cutting machine being brought to Syracuse.

In November of 1868, the statue was laid to rest near a tree behind Newell's farm. At the appointed time, Newell sent his unsuspecting workers to uncover the discovery of the century.

Hull's hoax grew bigger than his wildest dreams. He invested $2,600 in the building of the statue and as many as three thousand people a day at came to see the statue—first at an admission charge of twenty-five cents, then fifty cents, then a dollar.

This all became quite a business venture. People who saw it—whether believing it to be real or not—offered to buy the statue so they could profit from it. One guy wanted to put up the deed to his farm. Hull sold three-quarters of his shares in the giant to three Syracuse businessmen for $37,500. This meant the businessmen would begin to get a cut of the profits. The statue was a giant moneymaking machine.

Scientist after scientist came up with evidence that the statue was a hoax. They would expose simple facts—like why would a farmer have men dig on land that was already well irrigated? They said that the statue showed signs of soft tissue from the human body that would not leave a fossil trace if it was really as old as people were saying. They claimed over and over again that it was a poor fake.

The weird thing is no one wanted to believe it was a fake. Ninety-nine percent of the people who went to see it immediately believed it was not made by mere mortal hands. It seems the "truth is a matter of majorities."

The fact that the grooving of the underside of the statue looked like it was created by currents of water puzzled some, since gray limestone takes many years to groove. It added to the belief of many. Later it was realized that the statue was made of a soft sulfate of lime, a form of gypsum that can easily be grooved by even a fingernail. Mystery solved. Yet people kept believing and spending money to see the giant.

It was then that P.T. Barnum, the famous showman, offered to buy the statue for sixty thousand dollars. He was turned down since Hull and the gang weren't finished making money off of it. So Barnum did the only sensible thing a businessman would do. He built his own "Cardiff Giant" and claimed it was the "genuine" one, that Hull had sold it to him on the sneak. He claimed the statue Hull now had was a fake.

People came from all around to see this fake of a fake. P.T. Barnum's fake drew more people than the original fake! Upset at Barnum cutting in on his profits, Hull brought a lawsuit against him.

While the lawsuit was pending, stories started to unravel. A link was drawn between Hull and Newell. Hull had been hanging around the Newell farm a lot and people found out they were relatives. People remembered seeing a large box transported toward Newell's farm; the suspicious quarrying of a block of gypsum by Hull in Fort Dodge, Iowa, came under examination; and finally, the Chicago sculptors came forward and admitted they had built the statue for Hull.

Realizing the jig was up, Hull admitted in front of a courtroom full of people on February 2, 1870 that the whole thing was a hoax. The judge dismissed the case saying you couldn't sue for calling a statue a fraud when it was a fraud.

One of Hull's partners, David Hunnum, was annoyed that Barnum made money on a replica of a fake and Hunnum stated the famous words, "There's a sucker born every minute." However, it was Barnum who got the credit for those words.

For the next 130 years the two "Cardiff Giants" traveled around the country. Hull's original giant is on display at the Farmers Museum in Cooperstown, New York. A replica of the statue is at the Fort Museum in Fort Dodge, Iowa where the gypsum block originated. And once again, not to be outdone, P.T. Barnum's Cardiff Giant rests propped up in Farmington Hills, Michigan, in Marvin's Marvelous Mechanical Museum. The Cardiff Giant is one of the most notable hoaxes of all time.

204 Counts of Fraud
Unravel Tweed
· 1873 ·

Like sickening roaches, members of the Tweed Ring scattered as the newspapers shed light on and exposed them. The ringleader, William Magear "Marcy" Tweed, known simply as the Boss, was the Grand Sachem of the society known as Tammany Hall. He and his cohorts extorted approximately $200 million from the City of New York in the form of kickbacks from city contracts. Tweed and his gang made the city treasury their own, with every city contractor padding their bills for the Boss and his friends to take off the top. In a series of cartoons, Thomas Nast uncovered and highlighted the ring's corruption. The *New York Times* ran with the ball and the ringmasters did the only sane thing men with that much stolen money could do—they fled, taking their taxpayers' millions with them.

Tammany Hall started in 1789 for patriotic and fraternal support as the Society of St. Tammany. Through cunning and shrewd politics, the society turned into a powerful political weapon. The man who ruled Tammany ruled New York. Members of Tammany Hall got elected into the mayor's office and other high ranking positions.

Tweed, the Boss, was a big man in power and in stature, weighing in at a robust three hundred pounds. He stood six feet tall and had a ruddy complexion, a large prominent nose, small blue eyes, a beard, and was partially bald. He had a free and easy but coarse manner, with a great sense of humor that made him popular among blue collar New Yorkers. He realized his votes for the various political positions he ran for came from the working class, so he gave openly to charities and the poor. His strategy for ruling New York was simple, "Something for everyone" and "do it now." He allowed people to do as they wanted, even if it violated the blue laws. People could worship God with a glass of wine in hand even though New York law prohibited the sale of liquor on the Sabbath.

Like a master chess player, he positioned himself the king. He held many influential positions—superintendent of public works, county supervisor, state senator, Grand Sachem, chairman of the Democratic-Republican General Committee of the City of New York, president of the Guardian Savings Bank, member of the board of directors of the Harlem Gas Light Company, the Brooklyn Bridge Company, and the Third Avenue Railway Company, *and* the supervisor of the county court house—all at the same time!

Everyone was bought. The Boss held judges in his pockets like so many nickels and dimes, and he controlled reporters from thirty-seven different newspapers with payoffs to ensure favorable coverage. He even spread his influence to the heavens by giving city and state funds in the amount of $1,500,000 to the Catholic Church. He encouraged labor unions to organize and strike, assuring them he would be behind them. He gave unlimited borrowing power to the city to improve the sewage system, water supply, and bridges. He even used his influence to associate himself with tycoons Jay Gould and Jim Fisk by getting a law passed to legalize stock issued fraudulently by them, which helped them control the Erie Railroad over the tycoon Cornelius Vanderbilt. Because of this, Tweed got himself a seat on the Erie Railroad board.

But it all came tumbling down. Thomas Nast, a cartoonist for *Harper's Weekly*, drew a series of incriminating cartoons of Tweed and his henchmen's excessive borrowing, which drove Tweed mad because it infuriated the public. At the same time the *New York Times* received secret city and county receipts confirming the ring's actions from a discontented ex-sheriff, James O'Brien, who had been denied a large claim that he had against the city. On July 8, 1871, the *Times* published a long report of the fraud that had taken place and exposed ridiculous overspending such as "$175,000 for carpets for the court house, and $400,000 on safes."

The banks immediately refused to extend any further credit to the city as long as Tweed and company continued to run things. The banks demanded that the interest on the city bonds of $2,700,000 be paid by the first of November. With the Tweed Ring exposed, a judge had no choice but to issue an injunction forbidding the comptroller from issuing any other payments. This meant city workers would not get paid. Their paychecks had to go to paying back the city's interest on the bonds. Panic set in and crowds of angry workers gathered, demanding their pay.

The only choice was to get rid of the ring members pronto. Enter Samuel Tilden, the chairperson of the New York State Democratic Party, who went after Tweed with guns blazing. He formed a committee of seventy which gathered information to prove Tweed guilty beyond a shadow of a doubt.

As the evidence mounted, the guilty fled. The first to flee were those first indicted. Some members of the ring fled the country, some resigned, others "turned canary," and still others stuck with the proven method of bribery and intimidation. There were many indictments and few convictions. The stubborn Tweed remained in power until he was arrested on December 15, 1871, because money was traced from city contractors to Tweed's bank account. He hired David Fields, the best attorney of the day and a master at getting criminals off on technicalities. Fields delayed the trial for two years, hoping the public anger would cool off.

Suspiciously, once the trial took place, the jury, which consisted of many shady characters (including an ex-convict connected with Tweed), could not reach a verdict, and Tweed was set free.

Determined, Tilden immediately had Tweed arrested again on November 19, 1873 for signing six million dollars away in fraudulent contracts. Once again in the courtroom, Tweed remained calm and confident. His newly-appointed attorney, the prestigious John Graham, was known for his emotional outbursts in the courtroom—outbursts that could move even the most stubborn juror. But Tweed's calm turned to horror. His attorney broke into tears and never finished his closing argument. "Tweed hid his face in his hands and wept." He knew the verdict to come. When the untainted jury announced "guilty on 204 counts of fraud," the fearless Judge Davis slammed his hands on the desk and spoke of the audacity of the criminal with such force that the words echoed through every bone in Tweed's body. The judge, in his anger, gave Tweed a cumulative sentence of twelve years in prison with a fine of $12,750. Everyone was thrilled, thinking good had finally conquered evil.

But the conniving attorneys were not done with their handiwork. They won a release for Tweed on the grounds that a cumulative sentence was improper, and again the slippery Tweed was released from the cells of criminal imprisonment.

Anticipating their opponent's move, Tilden immediately had a civil suit slapped on Tweed in the name of the state, with bail set at 3 million dollars. Once again the Boss was behind bars in the Ludlow Street jail.

But with Warden Dunham as his friend, Tweed enjoyed a country club atmosphere. While he awaited trial for a year, Tweed would take afternoon drives with the warden, stopping at Tweed's home so he could dine with the missus.

Then one evening, during a peaceful dinner, Tweed excused himself to go upstairs and have a private moment with his wife. On December 4, 1875, he escaped right under the nose of his supposed keepers. Tweed's escape was a sensation. Reward posters offering ten thousand dollars were placed everywhere.

Like Elvis, in our time, Tweed was seen all over the world. Spottings took place from North Carolina to Georgia, Cuba and Canada, when all the time he was right in New York's sister state of New Jersey—in Palisades working as a laborer. In his absence, the jury brought damages against him for six million dollars. Panicked and desperate, he fled to Florida, then Cuba, and finally to Spain, where he worked as a seaman.

The authorities tracked him to Spain, but in an ironic twist of fate, they had no photos to offer the Spanish police for identification. However, they just happened to be carrying a copy of *Harper's Weekly*. Nast's cartoons once again did Tweed in. The police identified Tweed from the cartoons, and he was captured. He was returned to New York a beaten man on November 23, 1876, where he immediately resumed his residency at the Ludlow jail.

The very jail that Tweed had authorized the building of a couple of years prior was now his home. Tweed's desperation grew. Heart trouble, diabetes, and bronchitis overtook him.

In one last final negotiation, Tweed contacted Attorney General Charles Fairchild and offered a full confession of all his criminal activities in return for his release. But while Tweed was sailing the seas posing as a Spanish seaman, his main partner in crime, Peter Barr Sweeney, had beaten him to the punch and told Fairchild everything. Sweeney settled with the state for $400,000 and went free.

Even though no deal was made, Tweed wrote out a long, detailed confession of his ring's activities and gave it to Attorney General Fairchild. Fairchild returned the confession to Tweed, saying it was inaccurate and didn't contain enough information. But in fact, it contained *too much* information. Tweed's confession exposed an even greater scandal than the ring itself. Nearly half of the city and state officials were revealed as crooks. As the *Times* stated, "Could even Mr. Tilden afford to have Tweed's story told?"

In the end, Tweed died of pneumonia, in the Ludlow prison, a broken man abandoned by his friends. His dying words were "I hope Tilden and Fairchild are satisfied now." Of the estimated $200 million stolen while the Tweed Ring was in operation, only $894,525.44 was ever recovered. Only two of the many ring members were ever caught or punished. At the time of Tweed's death, sixteen suits were brought against various other members of the Tweed Ring. None came to trial.

Bridging Together
Two Wonders
of the World
• 1884 •

The new "eighth wonder of the world" opened with much fanfare in New York City in 1883. Its fate would eventually be intertwined with that of a living wonder, "the most famous beast alive."

In today's technological society, it's difficult to imagine why a new suspension bridge would be considered so miraculous. But up until the opening of the Brooklyn Bridge in 1883, suspension bridges experienced great failures due to mistaken theories and lack of technical information. At an alarming rate, suspended structures were collapsing from the very weight they were built to support, and winds were tearing them apart, leaving fear in the hearts of people who had to cross them. As recently as 1872, the Tacoma Narrows Bridge in Washington State had plummeted into the water from winds of only forty-two miles per hour.

The Brooklyn Bridge, spanning 1,595.5 feet, the longest in the world at the time, was able to withstand winds of over seventy miles per hour. The bridge was designed by John Augustus Roebling, the inventor of wire cable and an accomplished bridge builder. In 1867 he proposed the plan of building a unique bridge from Manhattan to Brooklyn and two years later, in 1869, construction finally began. Roebling touted the unprecedented use of steel, a stronger and lighter material than iron, which would provide unparalleled strength and stability to the bridge.

It's a wonder the bridge was ever built because it suffered many setbacks. The first was the death of John Augustus Roebling in 1869; he met with an untimely demise when a ferry toppled on him from a waterfront piling. His son, Washington Roebling, not wanting his father's dream to die with him, stepped in and took over the dangerous project.

The risk of fire was ever-present due to the use of welding equipment, and many of the workers suffered from decompression sickness, commonly known as the bends, or caisson disease, from being under high-pressure water for too long. Twenty of the six hundred men who worked on the bridge died during its construction; some are said to be buried in its walls. Roebling himself was paralyzed by the bends and had to continue to supervise the building through the use of a telescope from his bedroom. His wife, Emily Warren Roebling, took over supervision of the construction, working on site with the men, and ultimately saw the bridge through to completion.

On May 24, 1883, after fourteen harsh years of construction, the Brooklyn Bridge was officially opened. Many dignitaries attended the opening celebration, including the mayors of Brooklyn and New York City, Governor Grover Cleveland, United States senators, members of Congress, governors of other states, and President Chester A. Arthur.

The public was fascinated with this architectural wonder, but the bridge continued to have its share of tragedies. The Brooklyn Bridge became the focal point for men and women seeking fame and publicity. As if possessed, people began to jump off the bridge. Several people leaped to their deaths, including Robert E. Odlum, who jumped wearing a bright red swimming shirt. Another, Francis McCary, was the first suicide victim of the bridge. Other people jumped and lived. Larry Donovan, a newspaperman, jumped wearing a pair of baseball shoes. James Martin, a painter's assistant, fell accidentally and lived. Steve Brodie became a legend from his jump when pictures of him were posted all over the newspapers.

Fear of a new technology led to another Brooklyn Bridge tragedy. A week after the bridge opened, with approximately twenty thousand people crossing the structure at the time, a woman slipped and fell, causing another woman to scream. Within minutes, panic ensued. Someone shouted that the bridge was collapsing and people panicked and began to trample each other. Children were saved by being passed from person to person, eventually landing them on girders next to the cable-car tracks. In the end, the mass hysteria led to twelve people's deaths and many others were injured. Now, the bridge that was so glorified at its inception had become an object of apprehension and tragedy.

Always one to seize a moment of glory and publicity, P.T. Barnum, the famous circus showman, took it upon himself to alleviate people's fears and earn a bit of fame for himself and his prized elephant in the process.

Barnum had purchased Jumbo, a ten ton elephant, the largest elephant ever seen either in the wild or in captivity and a world wonder in his own right, due purely to a gross blunder by the superintendent of the Royal Zoological Gardens in London. He accepted Barnum's ten thousand dollar offer for Queen Victoria's favorite pet, thinking the elephant was too old to keep. The English public was outraged by the sale, even offering to buy

Jumbo back from Barnum and begging him to cancel the deal. The Royal Zoological Gardens came under severe attack for selling Jumbo, with the Prince of Wales and countless other statesmen and noblemen lamenting the loss of the star attraction and urging that the deal be canceled at any cost. Barnum knew he had made a shrewd deal and kept the elephant.

America rejoiced at the new addition to Barnum's circus, and after his debut on Monday, March 13, 1882, in Madison Square Garden, the fame of Jumbo brought in multitudes of people day after day and night after night wherever the circus traveled.

Two years later, on May 17, 1884, one year after the opening of the Brooklyn Bridge, Barnum sought, "in the interest of the dear public," to put an end to the fears concerning the supposed instability of the Brooklyn Bridge.

In one of the greatest publicity stunts ever, at 9:30 P.M. that evening, Barnum departed from the Courtland Street Ferry and marched up Broadway to the Brooklyn Bridge with his menagerie at his heels. Twenty-one elephants, seven camels, and ten dromedaries (one-humped Arabian camels trained for fast riding) snorted and shuffled their way across town, with the mighty Jumbo bringing up the rear. Thousands of cheering children and adults followed the procession, hooting and hollering "Hooray, it's Jumbo!" Broadway had never seen such a sight.

The mighty white elephant, ever a showman himself, waved his ears at his beloved fans as he approached the bridge, creating deafening cheers from people watching from their windows and rooftops.

With this one-of-a-kind stunt, the superintendent of tolls waived the bridge fare for Barnum and his cohorts since no one knew how much to charge an elephant or dromedary. This wondrous parade marched across the bridge amidst the arches, cables, and electric lights, creating an unforgettable sight.

On the other side of the bridge in Brooklyn, having completed their mission, the animals sauntered through enormous crowds to Tompkins and Fulton avenues, the location of

Barnum's showgrounds. Hoards of people cheered as the strength of the bridge was proven by the creative but simple act of marching thousands of tons of lovable animals across the bridge.

As P.T. Barnum once said, "Imagination is a gift, it is the incredible elixir of life." Roebling's technical talents and Barnum's imaginative spectacle forever bridged two wonders of the world.

The Lady in Green is High Maintenance
·1886·

Nothing could drench the spirit of the one million people waving the American flag and the Tricolor of France as they lined the four-mile parade route which started at Fifth Avenue and 57th Street then headed down Broadway to the Battery. On October 28, 1886, despite the cold rain, twenty thousand proud marchers—veterans, public officials, judges, governors, French-speaking socialites, Columbia and City College students, policemen and firemen from as far away as Baltimore—held their heads high as one band after another played the national anthems of France and the United States.

The gigantic celebration was for the long-awaited unveiling of the Statue of Liberty, originally named "Liberty Enlightening the

World." At 151 feet the statue was taller than any building in Manhattan and the tallest structure in the world at the time.

The last parade unit passed the presidential viewing stand at Madison Square Park near the Worth Monument shortly after one in the afternoon. The parade took about seven hours to pass a fixed point. President Grover Cleveland and his elite party of dignitaries from both France and the United States were proud at the valiant effort of the American and French citizens for making this symbol to commemorate the Declaration of Independence and international friendship possible. Everyone was dressed to the nines, some even in black evening wear, while all officers wore elaborate uniforms and medals of their rank.

But the statue was not always this well-received.

The thought of building a statue as a gift from France to America was conceived at an elite dinner party in the home of French historian and admirer of American democracy Edouard de Laboulaye in 1865. Laboulaye and his guests were discussing the friendship that had existed between the Americans and the French ever since France sent troops to fight on the side of the Americans during the revolution against England. One of his guests was a young, successful sculptor named Frederic-Auguste Bartholdi. Ever since his visit to Egypt in 1856, when he saw the Sphinx, he wanted to build something equally spectacular. With Laboulaye's persuasion, Bartholdi went to New York in June of 1871 to talk to President Ulysses S. Grant and other important Americans about a gift. Although the Americans were enthusiastic, it was up to France to make the first move.

Dedicated to the idea, Laboulaye formed the Franco-American Union, held all types of fundraising projects from lotteries to entertainment, and got 100,000 citizens of France to donate a total of $400,000. Bartholdi contributed twenty thousand dollars of his own money as well as the design of the statue. The statue was modeled after the Roman goddess Calisi, or *Libertas*, in Latin. This angered some Americans because the Roman Catholic Church had fought for many years to end the worship of idols by pagans, and here the French wanted to resurrect a defunct deity and make her into a colossus to place in New York Harbor.

The gift to America was also a public slap in the face to Napoleon III, who represented a monarchy. This "statue of liberty" was honoring a republic.

But these hard feelings were surmounted as the statue grew. The Americans had agreed to build and pay for a pedestal for the statue. So in America, Senator William Evarts and Secretary of the American Commission Richard Butler formed the Union League club to raise money. Money came in slowly and the very rich of the day, like the Vanderbilts, had not donated a dime. Joseph Pulitzer (of the Pulitzer Prize) used his newspaper, the *New York World* to raise money for the statue by writing, "It would be an irrevocable disgrace to New York City and the American Republic to have France send this splendid gift without our having to provide even so much as a landing place for it. We must raise the money!" He asked the rich citizens, such as the Vanderbilts and Jay Gould, to donate their hourly income. However, it was literally the American working people's donations of dimes and nickels that raised the money to build the pedestal. Eventually, $102,000 was donated.

Back in France, Bartholdi recruited the genius of Alexander-Gustave Eiffel (who later built the Eiffel Tower). Eiffel used his innovative bridge engineering technology to solve the problem of supporting the massive weight of the statue. The one hundred tons of copper used as the "skin" on the statue had to be secured in such a way that the statue would not buckle under its own weight. Eiffel introduced three separate structural systems bolted together to a central pillion to create a flexible skeletal structure made of 125 tons of steel. Eiffel's technique made it possible for the statue to sway three inches in fifty miles per hour or stronger winds and would allow the copper and steel to expand and retract in different temperatures without breaking.

Pierre-Gugene Secretan generously donated 350 pieces of 3/32-inch copper sheets that he purchased in Norway. The sheets were attached to the skeletal framework by a technique called Repousse Process. The idea of using copper as the skin was thought of by Viollet Le Duc, an engineer who died before the statue was started.

Meanwhile, across the sea, Richard M. Hunt was building an eighty-nine-foot granite pedestal on Bedloe Island (later renamed Liberty Island) on top of the abandoned, filled-in walls of an eleven-point, star-shaped military complex called Fort Wood.

On October 28, after the massive parade ended, a group of elite people attending by invitation only, excluding all but two women, boarded a boat and sailed over to Bedloe Island for the unveiling of the statue that had arrived in 214 separate crates. The reconstructed statue was bonded to the pedestal with two sets of steel anchorage beams that locked onto the primary skeleton of the statue, then ran down through the concrete pedestal to the foundation. The statue is so securely attached to its pedestal that the entire island would have to be turned over before the statue could fall.

At three in the afternoon, President Grover Cleveland reached Bedloe Island. Three hundred boats sat in the harbor waiting to blow their whistles at the appropriate time. One ship contained the New York Women's Suffragette Association. They were enraged that no American women were invited to the unveiling for "safety reasons." They screamed protests within earshot of those participating in the ceremonies, saying that if Lady Liberty would come to life, she would be appalled that only two women were invited on the island to celebrate.

The president marched up to the podium under a banner reading "Bartholdi and Liberty." The master of ceremonies, General Scholfield, opened the festivities, with a poem by John Greenleaf Whittier. Then William M. Evarts, chairman of the American Committee, known for his long-winded speeches, began to speak. The statue was to be unveiled immediately after he finished.

Bartholdi was waiting inside the statue's crown with a rope to remove the flag covering the face of the statue. At the signal of a boy waiting at the bottom, Bartholdi would pull the rope when Evarts stopped speaking. The boy, in his enthusiasm, mistook a pause in Evarts's speech to be the end, signaled Bartholdi, and the veil was dropped as thousands cheered. Ships in the harbor blasted their horns, guns saluted the statue, and Evarts sat down frustrated and unable to finish his speech.

When the pandemonium subsided, President Cleveland addressed the crowd and proclaimed, "We will not forget that Liberty has made her home here."

The remainder of the statue was unveiled in all its glory. Every part of the statue has symbolism. The seven spikes represent the seven seas and continents; the twenty-five windows in the crown represent the twenty-five natural minerals of earth; the toga represents the ancient republic of Rome; the torch represents enlightenment; the chains underfoot represent liberty crushing the chains of slavery; and the tablet held in the left hand of the statue inscribed with the date of July 4, 1776 is in reference to the day America proclaimed her independence from Britain.

Because of the dense fog and rain, the inaugural fireworks were delayed for three days. On November 1, 1886, at 7 P.M., rockets, bombs, and red, white, and blue flares lit the sky as Lady Liberty's torch was lit for the first time.

Elephant Arrested
for Swimming to
Quogue
· 1904 ·

It started out like any other summer adventure—a midnight swim with three buddies. But in this case the buddies were amusement park elephants escaping from Luna Park, one of Coney Island's most glamorous funland centers in the early 1900s, to head towards Quogue, Long Island. Perhaps they wanted a change of scenery or were just tired of working for peanuts. The unidentified elephants leaped into the New York bay and began a vigorous six-mile swim.

Somewhere along the way, the three could not agree as to the best route to Quogue, so they separated and decided to go it alone. One nautical elephant detoured and started to head toward New Dorp, Staten Island.

This began one of the most memorable days in New Dorp history. Having abandoned his synchronized swimming with his partners, our Elephant X was practicing the crawlstroke, seemingly enjoying the early morning sea water.

At the same time, Frank Krissler and a friend had just arrived in New Dorp after work and decided to engage in their favorite leisurely sport—fishing. At about 4 A.M., amidst thick fog, they rowed some quarter of a mile offshore and cast their lines as they had done many times in the past, expecting the usual catch of fluke and flounder.

When "suddenly across the still waters there came an unearthly sound. It had too much volume, they said for a groan, was too loud for a bellow, and too deep for a siren," reported the *New York Times*. But this was only the beginning. The first sound had barely died down when out from the mist came another more powerful and eerie sound than before. What was more frightening was that the tremendous sound was headed their way.

"Rhinoceros," howled Krissler. (Although why a land jungle animal would come to mind to an experienced fisherman in the middle of the ocean is a mystery.) "Whale," yelled his friend. And at that very moment, while they were playing deep-sea charades, "The huge Thing" and the fishermen spotted each other. Alarmed at seeing a gigantic mass in the water, Frank and friend turned the boat around and started rowing away at a warp speed that would have made Mario Andretti proud.

The chase was on. Krissler and friend rowed for their lives, and the elephant followed in hot pursuit. The faster they rowed, the faster it followed. There was no losing him. As they rowed onto the beach, it was right behind them.

Finally they turned and saw it was not some mythological serpent but a docile, misguided, somewhat frightened and waterlogged elephant. The three of them stood there staring at each other as two more fishermen arrived. Not having much experience with a wayward elephant, the four decided to lasso him around the tusks. He submitted without resistance. The fishermen led him like an oversized poodle on a leash to the "protective" custody of the police.

As the shackled elephant entered the precinct flanked by his captors, officers were aghast at the size of the perpetrator.

Showing no sympathy for his ignorance of the law, the unidentified elephant was booked for vagrancy and placed on the police blotter. The elephant "took the Fifth" and didn't have much to say on the matter. Was there a jail cell big enough to hold him? He was locked up in a stable normally reserved for the horses of the mounted police and provided with the usual hay and water.

The news of this unusual captive spread like wildfire to the New Dorp townsfolk. Hundreds of people gathered outside the jail and demanded to see the prisoner. Some wanted to know if he had been read his rights. As they hung around the station waiting for the prisoner's release, the townspeople each had their own stories to tell about the aquatic elephant. Each story, just like any good fisherman's tale, differed greatly except for the fact that the beast swam the six miles from Brooklyn to Staten Island.

Police allowed the crowd to gaze at the harmless beast through the town jail bars. One officer, referring to their biggest catch ever, stated, "Press agent or no press agent, we got him, and we are going to keep him till a bondsman shows up."

The police stuck to their word because the poor elephant stayed in jail, with the throng outside, until 7:30 P.M. when finally a spokesperson from Luna Park showed up to claim the elephant. An elaborate explanation was made by the spokesperson, who stated that the elephant was a shoot-the-chutes performer.

After much red tape and many signed papers, the prisoner was released into the spokesperson's custody. Witnessing this and desperate for their freedom, other prisoners claimed to be part of the Luna Park show.

The elephant was led down the boulevard, put on a ferry, and taken across the bay back to Coney Island. The *New York Times* trumpeted the amusing tale with the banner headline "Elephant Lands in Jail for Swimming Narrows."

On the ferry, the elephant was searching the waters for his two companions, who were by now sunning themselves on the sandy beaches of Quogue. Dismayed . . . not even a postcard.

Spectacular
100 m.p.h.
Vanderbilt Cup Race
· 1904 ·

Signs were posted on telegraph poles and fences all over Long
Island by the Automobile Association of America and the Board
of Supervisors of Nassau County:

> An automobile race over a distance of between 250 and
> 300 miles will be held for the William K. Vanderbilt Jr.
> Cup on Saturday October 8. The start will be at
> Westbury at daylight. All persons are warned against
> using the roads between the hours of 5 A.M. and 3 P.M.
> Officers will be stationed along the road to prevent
> accidents. . . . All persons are cautioned against

allowing domestic animals or fowl to be at large. Children unattended should be kept off the roads. . . . Chain your dogs and lock up your fowl. To avoid danger, don't crowd into the road.

And with that the scene was set for the start of the first international race on American soil on July 7, 1904.

Twenty-five-year-old millionaire sportsman William Kissam Vanderbilt Jr. had set the world's speed record in 1902 with a speed of 76.09 miles per hour in his Mors racer and the 1904 record in his Mercedes, which had clocked at 92.80 miles per hour in Europe. He loved the adrenaline rush and the excitement racing stirred in the crowds. He also noticed that racing competitions forced the foreign car industry to improve its technology. They built cars lighter and faster. He wanted the same thing for the American automobile industry.

He persuaded the Automobile Association of America (AAA), of which he was a founder, to promote a classic, international, closed-circuit race to be held in Long Island. He promised to sponsor the event and to provide a thirty-one-inch-high Tiffany cup made of 481 ounces of sterling silver.

At first the local townspeople did not want the race. Some felt it was dangerous. Some felt it was foolish. As one preacher from a church in Brooklyn proclaimed, "Men of today are choking themselves on luxuries. Oh, the degradation of such a scene! . . . As revolting as bartering Christ's garments for a few pieces of silver." Others protested because it was against the law. American law forbade the closure of roads to the general public and the use of federal troops to do crowd control. Some just didn't want to be inconvenienced. Farmers were prepared to block the event with guns in hand and slow-moving vehicles to aggravate the racers. But as the grandstand started to be built, the potholes filled in, the dirt roads smoothed over and heavily oiled, and tons of sod and sand deposited to grade and bank vital curves and sharp turns, excitement started to grow. Protesters started to think of the profits that the race could bring to the town. The race became a highly anticipated event.

The rules for the race were straightforward. Cars were to have a four cylinder motor and could weigh no more than 2,204 pounds and not less than 881. Each car and all of the parts in it had to be manufactured in the country it represented. During the race, the car had to carry two men weighing at least 132 pounds each. They had to run ten laps over a route totaling not less than 250 miles of open road, but not more than 300. The winner would be determined by a calculation based on speed to miles. The race was open to any clubs recognized by either the AAA or the Automobile Club of France. No country could enter more than ten cars. The cup was to be held by the club, not an individual. The acceptance deadline for the race was September 8, 1904.

The start of the race was near Hicksville. The course ran along Jericho Turnpike through Mineola to Queens and then back through Hempstead along the Beth Page Turnpike to Plain Edge, where a turn was made north along Massapequa Road and then back through Hicksville again to the finish line. The course had eleven bad corners, including a complete U-turn and many curves and S-turns. It also had two steep hills. The race would be a grueling challenge for the racers and their cars.

Eighteen contestants entered and qualified—five in the German team, six in the French team, two in the Italian team, and five in the American team. No country wanted to risk not being represented in the first American race. The world's best drivers were entered.

The unusual and colorful cars and their daredevil drivers started arriving in Mineola, Garden City, and Hempstead. The Garden City Hotel became the communication center for the AAA club to announce the famous arrivals and keep the press and the public excited.

Like anxious kids waiting to open their Christmas packages, the crowds gathered to watch the practice runs around their local streets. Breakdowns, minor accidents, tires blowing out, and steering wheels freezing and causing drivers to swerve out of control all added to the building anticipation.

The night before the race electricity was in the air. The hotels, inns, taverns, boarding rooms, and farm houses in the area were filled to capacity with enthusiastic sports fans. Thousands of drivers were trying to make their way out of New York City and cars were lined chrome-to-chrome (since bumpers weren't invented yet). Ferries from 34th Street to Long Island City were leaving every ten minutes. Bicycles, buggies, farm wagons, carriages, and touring cars clogged the roads of Queens County. Campsites dotted the course with their bonfires, makeshift picnics, and parties. The Waldorf Astoria stayed open all night for the fifty-two breakfasts that had been scheduled between two and seven o'clock in the morning. Everyone was preparing for the first running of the Vanderbilt Cup Race.

At dawn, on the fresh, clean morning of October 8, 1904, William Vanderbilt Jr. ran down the steps of the Garden City Hotel, jumped into his sparkling white Mercedes racing car, and headed to the grandstand on Jericho Turnpike in Westbury where he was to referee the race.

Technical advisors, starters, timers, judges, press, program officials, and the superintendents of the grandstand were all in place. The New York & New Jersey Telephone Company was handling the communication system around the course.

The grandstand had a tall pole with a large American flag flying proudly on top. Over the heads of the judges were the smaller flags representing the countries of the racers. In front of the grandstand were signs with the words "START" and "FINISH LINE" in bold, black letters. The grandstand announcements were to be barked out over a leather-covered megaphone, and the Nassau Hospital was on standby for any injuries.

Twenty-five thousand spectators—businessmen in suits and stiff collars, other men in knickerbockers, driving caps, and gauntlets, and women in long skirts and short, puffed-sleeved jackets and high-collared blouses—were waiting all along the course, ready to be a part of history. In almost every hand was a racing program with the headline "Devil Cars Will Race" boldly printed.

The eighteen contestants were all lined up and rolling out of their pits. Only the heads of the drivers in their goggles and leather caps could be seen. Everybody had drawn a number to see when they would start the race. The number thirteen was omitted from the drawing because it was thought to bring bad luck.

The starter, with his crisp new flag in hand, stood ready for the timer's signal. At exactly 6 A.M., the clock began, the starter yelled "Go" and the first racer let out his clutch smoothly and with thunderous roaring and flames leaping from the open exhaust pipe, he was off. Campbell, with the number one stenciled on his red Mercedes, had begun the race.

As the number two car, driven by a man named Gabriel, was given the signal, a small steam touring car carelessly headed out onto the track. Frantic waving and the announcer's stern reprimands over the megaphone got the car out the way. One by one, every two minutes, a car was given the signal as the crowd tingled with excitement and cheered for their favorite driver. Car number seven was driven by American George Heath. Ironically, Alfred G. Vanderbilt's Fiat had broken down, leaving only seventeen cars in the race.

The first lap was the most grueling and confusing one for the drivers. Some cars overtook others on narrow roads; other cars fell back because of the time it took to make repairs. Wide-eyed spectators sat in trees and in the road itself to get a glimpse of the drivers. As the first driver came hurtling into the stretch at the end of the first lap, he appeared to be headed right for the crowd. People cried out, "Car coming! Car coming!" as others jumped into nearby bushes and ditches for safety. With each car thereafter came the familiar cry of "Car coming!," and several crazed people decided to see how close they could get to the passing racers without getting hit.

Quickly the laps took victims. George Arents Jr., driving a Mercedes, blew a tire. The rim caught in a trolley track, the car overturned, and the passenger, his mechanic, was killed instantly.

Another Mercedes driver took off after stopping for a repair, forgot that his mechanic was under the car, and ran over him.

One car was almost hit as it dashed across the railroad tracks in front of an oncoming train.

By the second lap, only nine cars remained. Then even more drivers had to quit. One car's Simplex metal frame began to sag more and more until finally it dragged on the ground and caused the car to slow to a pathetic crawl, then stop.

Finally, it was down to two drivers, Heath and Clement, vying for the lead. The crowd had now grown to 100,000. Vanderbilt was standing at the grandstand with the checkered flag in hand ready to declare a winner. Amidst great cheers and shouting, Heath crossed the finish line first. Clement followed only one minute, twenty-eight seconds behind. George Heath, in his ninety horsepower Panhard, had a net time of 5:26:45, with an average speed of 52.4 miles per hour. Heath won the first American Vanderbilt cup race.

The air was charged; the crowd was ecstatic. With the exception of the fatal accident and the unruly crowd, the race was a successful international sporting event, giving excitement and a memorable experience to thousands.

Vanderbilt Cup races were held in 1904, 1905, 1906, 1908, 1909 but ended in 1910 because of too many spectator casualties. Faster cars resulted in more accidents, and blood flowed like water. The crowds grew too large to control, and things got completely out of hand when a mechanic crashed and was killed, and before the body stopped rolling, it was stripped naked by souvenir hunters.

Wall Street Lays an Egg
·1929·

Thousands upon thousands of thrill seekers and zombie-like investors gathered on Wall Street outside the New York Stock Exchange in the early hours of Tuesday, October 29, 1929, waiting for the fatal blow. Police and detectives had been sent in to keep the crowd from storming the entrance. Tension and fear were in the air as everyone waited for ten o'clock to come and the opening trading gong to sound and reveal the fates of those outside. This was Black Tuesday—the most destructive day in stock market history.

Like waves in an ocean during a storm, gathering strength one by one, each plunge was taking its toll. On October 24, Black Thursday, the stock market took a devastating plunge and wiped out many private investors. The following Monday, October 28, it nose-dived again and businesses went bankrupt. Then came the final wipeout. The tidal wave crashed on October 29, 1929, devastating the economy and hurtling the country into the Great Depression with such force that it took a full decade to recover.

The bull market, the unequal distribution of wealth with two hundred corporations controlling almost half of all corporate assets mainly in the automotive and radio industry, and the boom of the Roaring Twenties, when it was a "craze" to play the market, set the stage for the final crash. Stock prices were artificially high but little guys could speculate alongside the big boys by purchasing stocks on margin, meaning they could buy stocks without the money to purchase them. They could put a little money down and buy the rest on credit from their brokers. With potential returns of 3,400 percent, everyone wanted to play. Stocks themselves became the collateral.

All this pushed stock prices artificially higher. People invested their bank accounts, treasury bonds, and life savings to make a "killing on the market." As long as stocks were rising, everything was fine. This enormous amount of unsecured consumer debt left the market unbalanced. Eventually margins become due. Someone had to pay the piper.

In 1929, the stock market began to move up and down like a roller coaster. The Coolidge Administration's attitude had been laissez-faire—"let things be." No one wanted to intervene and be blamed for causing a crash. Some smart investors began to pull out, knowing that the economy could not stay on the upswing forever. Wall Street wizard Bernard Baruch felt that "the condition of the market could be measured by its wild fluctuations, followed by assurances from every direction that all was well. But I had heard this lullaby before." He told Will Rogers to sell, which he did. Ed Barrow, president of the New York Yankees, told his players to get out of the market as soon as possible. By March President Herbert Hoover had the Federal Reserve Board meeting every day behind closed doors to discuss what could be done about the market and the economy.

On that fateful day, October 29, brokers fidgeted nervously, some just stared as if hypnotized as their world collapsed around them. In the first thirty minutes of trading, huge chunks of stocks were sold—fifty thousand shares at a clip of some of the largest corporations. Chrysler, General Electric, and Standard Oil were dumped like unwanted garbage by the rich and by large institutions. The price of U.S. Steel, one of the largest companies at the time, slid down and down at a dizzying pace. RCA plummeted from $110 and couldn't get takers at $26 per share. AT&T went from $310 to $204, wiping out Clarence Mackay, who according to the *Wall Street Journal* "suffered the greatest reversal of fortune of any individual speculator in America."

Those brokers trying to hold on were frightened and frantic. One trader cracked under the pressure and "ran screaming like a lunatic from the floor of the exchange."

By noon, 8,350,000 shares of stock had been sold and bought, more than any other time in the stock market's one-hundred-year trading history. Because of the extremely low prices, stock brokers violated normal trading practices, not to mention exchange regulations by delaying many transactions, hoping for a more reasonable bid to appear. But, as someone said, it was like "trying to stem the falls of Niagara."

Meanwhile, Mayor Jimmy Walker spent his lunch hour at a convention of motion picture exhibitors at the Hotel Astor. He was pleading with them, "Show pictures that will reinstate courage and hope in the hearts of the people. Give them a chance to forget their financial losses on the stock market and look with hope to the future. . . . The morale of the people must be maintained, and you can do it."

But people couldn't take it. After suffering a loss of $124,000, the vice president of the Earl Radio Corporation jumped from an eleventh floor window of the Hotel Lexington and smashed to the ground on Lexington with a note that read, "We are Broke."

The Marx Brothers were opening a one-week run of *Animal Crackers* in Baltimore. Shortly before the curtain went up, Harpo received a wire stating, "Forced to sell all holdings unless receive check for $15,000 to cover margins." Groucho Marx was so depressed he refused to go onstage. No one could convince him to leave the dressing room. A stand-in had to take his place.

Out of the news tickers came urgent messages to try to calm fears. "Federal Reserve Board in Session in Washington . . . Telegraph, telephone, and cable systems carrying record volume of communications to Wall Street from around the globe . . . Leading wire houses say worst is over."

But the truth was that almost every investment trust had gone bankrupt. Men and women tried to force their way into brokerage offices to follow the ticker tapes. Financially demolished families wandered around aimlessly in hotel lobbies as if in a trance. Yet stock prices kept falling.

The governing committee of the stock exchange assembled shortly after noon beneath the trading floor in a cramped, smoked-filled room, trying to decide what to do. They debated closing the market for the rest of the day but decided to keep it open. Some had a glimmer of hope, thinking the carnage would stop at some point. It didn't.

A businessman in Rhode Island dropped dead in his broker's office of a heart attack as he watched the ticker tape. A Kansas man shot himself in the chest twice, knowing he could never repay his debts.

Between 2:30 and 3:00 in the afternoon, there was a slight buying surge, as some thought it was a great opportunity to pick up blue chip stocks at an incredibly low price. Institutions tried to make a heroic effort to restore some faith by buying stock. But it was too late.

By 5:32 P.M., after the final words "Good Night" had run across the board, nine billion dollars worth of securities values had vanished in the space of five hours. The estimated total loss for the nation was fifteen billion dollars; an astronomical 16,410,000 shares had been traded in one day. The thirty leading industrials had lost forty percent of their value.

The headline in *Variety* the next day read, "Wall St. Lays an Egg." "Bank and trust stock prices crumble in record trading: crowds at tickers see fortunes wane," read the *New York Times*.

Comedian Eddie Cantor, at a Jewish Theatrical Guild Luncheon the previous Sunday, had joked, "If the stock market goes any lower, I know thousands of married men who are going to leave their sweethearts and go back to their wives. As for myself, I am not worried. My broker is going to carry me, he and three other pall bearers." After the crash, Cantor was left with $60 in his pocket, and he owed $285,000 to Manufacturers Trust Company. Irving Berlin was broke after the crash, and Harpo Marx liquidated every asset except his harp and croquet set to pay his debts.

The crash created a domino effect. Everyone lost their confidence in the economy's stability. The rich stopped spending money on luxury items. The middle class stopped buying on credit for fear of losing their jobs and the fear that they could never pay back the interest. Industrial production levels fell, since there was less buying. People were laid off. To protect whatever was left of the nation's business, tariffs were imposed and foreigners then stopped buying American products. More jobs were lost, and more stores closed. Banks and factories closed. By 1930, five million people were unemployed. The downward spiral affected the entire industrial world. The Great Depression had begun.

Dumped Farmers
Dump Milk
· 1939 ·

The tension had been mounting for years, with outbursts of violence and mass arrests taking place all over the Midwest. Then the giant wave hit New York. By 1931, the price of milk had fallen so low that thousands of "independents" and farmers who supplied small dealers could not even pay for the bare necessities of life. Dairymen were threatened with the loss of their farms and their homes in which their meager life savings were invested. They had to strike back as a matter of survival. And strike back they did.

But these unorganized strikes of rage were basically ineffective in bringing down the three powerful, giant milk corporations: United States Dairy Products Company, Borden's Condensed Milk Company, and Sheffield Farms Milk Company. Together, these three companies handled two-thirds of the fluid milk sold in New York City. The farmers needed to regroup and come up with a new plan.

In 1939, the Dairy Farmers Union (DFU), under the leadership of its creator Archie Wright, organized one of the largest and most successful milk strikes in New York State history. Wright, a former organizer for the Industrial Workers of the World Union (IWW), had left that position and returned to his father's thirty-nine-cow farm in Heuvelton, New York. Seeing the plight of the small farmer, on October 15, 1936, he organized the Dairy Farmers Union at the Town Hall in Canton, New York. From then on, he passionately defended the rights of farmers with the skills of a seasoned politician and the strategy of a four-star general.

Wright knew that dairy farming was the dominant industry in a large part of rural upstate New York. He also knew that dairy farmers had the support of their local communities. They represented the common man. And he knew that the small farmers' direct-action protests had been essentially unsuccessful. As Wright put it, "Farm organizations don't make a milk strike. A milk strike is something like an earthquake. You can't even set the day. The farmers are the people who make a milk strike."

Wright wanted to harness their energy in a "Strong, militant Union of enlightened farmers" who would use their control over milk production and the threat of disrupting the industry as a way to gain the political and economic power that they so desperately needed if they were going to not get wiped out by the big three. His plan was set. By June of 1939, the DFU had fourteen thousand members—a force to be reckoned with.

The reason the farmers were striking was simple: pure economics and survival. There were four main factors involved. First, the Depression had lowered prices. In 1931 farmers were getting $2.25 for one hundred pounds of milk; in 1933 they were only getting ninety-nine cents. Second, farmers had used technology to increase milk production. Third, the farmers' cost for transporting milk had not declined, and fourth, the big three companies had agreements among themselves to only work with other major producer cooperatives. The big three had sixty-six thousand dairy farmers under contract between them. This left out the small independents who supplied one-third of the milk sold both in New York City and outside the metro area. The big three had to carry excess fluid milk capacity to sell during the winter months when milk production was low and consumption was high. Storage costs were passed on to consumers. In contrast, independents did not have to carry a surplus, so their prices were lower but their distribution was limited. The big three and the independents were locked into a constant price war. A milk board had been set up in 1933 to regulate prices but it consistently favored the big three.

Over the years leading up to the big milk strike, Wright gained public support for the DFU by never cutting off the supply of milk to the army, orphanages, or hospitals. The union was becoming known for its "100% effective strikes staged without bloodshed, without tumult."

The stage was now set. On August 3, 1939, two hundred DFU members met in Canton, New York, and voted to strike unless they received an average price of $2.35 per hundred pounds of milk. That same day DFU members all over New York met and the results were the same—strike. Farmers in LaFargeville, Lowville, Tritown, Canton, Jefferson County, Mohawk and the Hudson River Valley—a total of 14,962 members—voted to begin picketing and diverting milk in three days.

Wright emphasized organization, strategy, and non-violence during the strike to keep public support. But people feared the violence that had occurred during other strike Actions. DFU opponents, including the Milk Producers Bargaining Agency, used this fear and spread the word that "farm families were guarding [their] homes tonight in fear of armed invaders." They also accused the DFU of being an "out and out CIO Communist Movement." But despite those efforts, the milk farmers had an impact—after just one day of striking, the DFU quickly cut the New York City fluid milk supply by thirty percent.

The strategy of the DFU was simple: gather the masses of farmers and their supporters and station them outside the gates of local milk plants. The picketers blocked off every road leading to the targeted milk plants, as well. Thousands of farmers lined the streets as delivery attempts were made. They approached drivers at their windows and "talked" with them. The sheer number of strikers dissuaded many non-striking farmers from delivering their milk.

It wasn't really hard to convince the "co-op farmers" and the non-DFU farmers to join the strike. In times of crisis, people join with others they feel are in the same position. There was deep discontent in the "rank and file." Many non-DFU farmers joined the strike by refusing to deliver milk or by arranging for the DFU picket to dump their milk. The co-op farmers said they could not make deliveries because of the threat of violence. This allowed them to support their fellow farmers and appear to want to meet their contractual obligations at the same time.

To deal with the angry non-strikers who wanted to bust up the pickets, DFU farmers placed planks embedded with large nails in nearby roads where they were picketing, as a second line of defense. They also set up "flying squadrons" made up of several DFU members. These squadrons were large, stake-rack trucks patrolling county roads in search of non-striking farmers attempting to deliver milk. The flyers confiscated any milk they found and dumped it or sent it to another part of New York.

A mysterious fire at a local dairy barn in Heuvelton blazed as an ominous warning to the few remaining farmers who persisted in breaking through picket lines and delivering their milk. By the strike's third day, the DFU had a firm grip on New York City's milk supply, cutting it by sixty percent.

Women also played an essential role in the strike, not only as union officers but as very persuasive picketers for the DFU. They were credited with turning back more milk than the men. Men were less likely to run over a woman blocking the road than another male farmer. As the *Ogdensburg Journal* reported, "Women seemed to be just as active as the men here . . . and more than one officer's face turned crimson at the remarks tossed their way by the fairer sex."

Many women also took on bigger work loads, churning thousands of pounds of butter—sometimes in their washing machines, and milking more cows, while the men were out picketing. Many non-DFU men kept their milk home because their wives pleaded with them to stick by the other farmers.

Police officers called in to control the strike were put in an awkward position. If they sided with their friends and neighbors, as they often did, the milk companies would go over their heads, calling their friends in government to mobilize local police.

The big three didn't stand idle during the strike. The Sheffield Farms plant had police escorts standing guard when milk was delivered. The Dairy Farmers Union retaliated by greasing the train rails leading out of the plant which delayed the departure of the daily milk trains. After the fifth night of picketing by the DFU, the manager of the Sheffield plant along with two employees attacked a picketer with a baseball bat. This led to two days of angry rioting by the DFU, despite strict instructions by Wright to avoid violence. Union members threw rocks at windows and destroyed Sheffield company property. In turn, a company guard shot and wounded a local farmer.

Enough was enough. New York City Mayor Fiorello LaGuardia, hoping to avoid a milk shortage altogether, stepped in and asked for representatives from the DFU, major co-ops, and dealers to send representatives to a conference at the World's Fair grounds in Queens.

On the ninth day of the strike, a settlement drawn up by LaGuardia called for a pact for dealers to recognize the DFU as a powerful regional dairy farmers' organization and to pay $2.15 per hundred-weight for all milk purchased between August 25 and October 31, 1939—a forty-five percent increase. The pact was ratified at a DFU convention in Utica, New York.

The grassroots Dairy Farmers Union emerged on top. Archie Wright had proven that farmers were not "ignorant and back-wards," and that when pushed, they could successfully fight back. As one sign read, "If we all pull together, and nobody kicks, we will show the dealers, we are not Hicks."

In celebration of the farmers' victory, many parades with bands and balloons were held. In Canton, New York, a mock funeral even took place, complete with two coffins and fake mourners dressed in black. One coffin was for the Dairymen's League and the other for the "milk monopoly."

The three milk giants fought back quickly. They spread propaganda and poured thousands of dollars into a campaign claiming Archie Wright was a communist. Eventually people started to question whether it might be the truth, and although Wright fought hard and long, he was forced to resign. Without its leader, the DFU, one of the nation's most powerful farmer organizations, disbanded.

The FBI's Most Wanted Criminal
· 1950 ·

The streets were deserted at six o'clock on the freezing morning of March 9, 1950, in the residential town of Westerleigh, Staten Island. Frost lay quietly on the lawns, and the only sound was that of a man pulling out of his driveway on his way to his job at the Manufacturers Trust Company Bank in Sunnyside, Queens. That man was Willie Sutton, the most notorious criminal in America and number one on the FBI's "Most Wanted" list.

The night before, Willie Sutton had done what he always did before a big job. His m.o. *(modus operandi)* was to disguise himself. He dyed his hair ash blond and picked out a padded suit that would conceal the shape of his body. He wasn't going to wear a uniform. Willie had acquired several uniforms over the years by presenting bogus letterheads to people that read, "Waverly School of Art and Drama." In no time at all, he had several costume donations in his "actor's closet." In every other job Willie Sutton had pulled off, he had disguised himself as either a policeman, postman, fireman, Western Union messenger, carpenter, or even a window washer. To Willie, a uniform was a badge of admission. It worked like a charm. He would waltz in and out of banks, jewelry stores, and insurance companies without suspicion. He acted like he owned the place. This time was different. Willie was going to rob the bank without a uniform, and the additional challenge excited him even more.

As Willie stood before the mirror that morning, staining his skin a dark olive, thickening his eyebrows with mascara, and broadening his nostrils with hollowed-out corks, he had questioned his sanity. He was forty-nine years old and had been a fugitive for three years. He had plenty of money stashed away. If he was caught, he would go back to prison for the rest of his life. They didn't even have to catch him for another bank robbery—the sentence would be mandatory, no ifs, ands or buts, because of the other crimes for which he was wanted. But against all logic, he was determined to get this bank his way, even though there was a good chance he'd get caught. It was an irresistible challenge and he loved it.

Satisfied with his appearance, Willie was ready.

For three weeks, he had cased the bank located on busy Queens Boulevard. Willie loved working in crowds for three reasons: the more there was going on in the street, the less likely people were to look in the bank; the thousands of people passing made it easier to case the place, and if something should go wrong no sensible cop would fire shots into a crowd.

Manufacturers Trust was an ideal hit. The guard, Weston, arrived at 8:30 A.M., the time-lock was released at 9:00, and the doors were open to the public at 10:00. Every other bank opened at 9:00, so at Manufacturers Trust, Willie had extra time to operate. He had observed and watched the arrivals of the sixteen employees and even of the mailman. He knew people were creatures of habit, even himself, especially when it comes to time. He also knew the pecking order at the bank. The most important person, Mr. Hoffman, the bank manager and combination holder, arrived last at 9:01 A.M. Willie planned his crime around the schedules of the employees.

After getting ready on the morning of the job, Willie went to Manhattan to pick up his first partner in crime, Tommy "Mad Dog"

Kling, whom he had met in prison. Tommy was wearing four-inch-high shoes as part of his disguise. The two drove over to a garage just off Queens Boulevard where they had stashed their stolen car and met John DeVenuta, the third man in.

DeVenuta had stolen a new, out-of-state Pontiac, and under an assumed name Willie had bought a wrecked car for about one hundred dollars. He dumped the wreck, switched the plates, and forged a registration, in case they got stopped for a minor traffic violation. Willie had gotten the rubber stamp that made the registration official. With the getaway car in order, they headed to the bank.

Right on schedule, at exactly 8:30, Weston, the guard, bought his newspaper at the corner of 45th Street and Queens Boulevard and headed to the bank with his nose buried in the paper. Willie followed so closely behind him, that he practically could have been his shadow. As Weston put the key in the lock and pushed open the door, Willie slid in right behind him undetected. Weston closed the door, locked it, turned around, and was shocked to see Willie standing before him. Willie had already taken Weston's pistol out of the holster and was pointing it at him. Willie laid out the plan for Weston and told him there would be no problem if he cooperated fully. The trembling Weston, persuaded by the gun in his side, agreed to cooperate.

The first part of the plan was for Weston to let Willie's partners in and give them a grand tour of the bank—the conference room, alarm system, the whole works.

Then Kling and DeVenuta set up seventeen chairs in two rows facing the vault. The setup of the chairs was blocked from the vision of passers by on the street by a five-foot wooden partition topped by a foot and a half of frosted glass. Then they waited for the bank employees to arrive.

To prevent Weston from bolting out the door as he let the employees in, Willie chained Weston's ankle to a radiator in the vestibule just inside the door with a dog chain he had brought.

As employees arrived, they were escorted by Kling to the waiting chairs where DeVenuta was stationed to watch them. As he brought them to the chairs, Kling explained very calmly that the bank was being robbed. Willie was very much into the psychological aspects of robbery. He understood that knowing what is happening has a calming effect on people. Frightened people do foolish things; he wanted them to listen, not to be scared. Willie even joked with them to ease the tension. "Don't worry folks, it's only money. And it isn't your money."

Willie was also careful to let the workers know that he was in total control; he knew the bank and all the lingo. Again, this gave the employees a feeling of ease. The assistant manager, Mr. Sands, arrived right on time. When the chairs were about full, Mr. Hoffman, the bank manager, arrived. Of all days, Hoffman decided to be four minutes late. When Hoffman finally showed up and saw the employees sitting around in chairs, he quickly figured out what was happening.

Willie knew the handling of the manager was the most critical part of the operation. The employees had nothing to lose; it wasn't their money. The guard was deflated the moment his gun was taken, but the manager was an important player in Willie's plan. He was the head honcho and the man who had to make the decision to open the vault. So, Willie gave him a psychological out.

Mr. Hoffman, you're the bank manager. We know all about this place. . . . You have the first three numbers of the combination and Mr. Sands, your assistant manager, has the last three. You are going to open the vault for us. If you give me any trouble, I want you to know that some of these here employees of yours will be shot. I don't want you to have any false illusions about that. Now perhaps you don't care about your safety, but the health of these here employees of yours are your responsibility. If anything happens to them the blame will be yours, not mine.

Having said this, he put the manager in a position where he had to act responsibly on behalf of his employees. He could save face because he had no choice.

Hoffman and Sands opened the vault. The money was not just lying around on the floor loose like a million-dollar lottery grab bag. It was in smaller compartments, or mini-safes, that were also locked. Hoffman and Sands unlocked these compartments and the robbers filled their bags. Hoffman tried to avoid the reserve compartment which usually contained the most money. Willie had him open it and for some unknown reason, it was empty. After they had cleaned out all the compartments, Willie estimated that they had stolen about $150,000.

With the job done, Willie led the gang down to the conference room while Kling and DeVenuta got the getaway car. Willie made his parting speech to the bank employees reminding them that it wasn't their money and that it would be replenished in a couple of hours. He told them he was going upstairs to check on something with his partners and he'd be back in a few minutes. He left and never came back.

Outside the bank, the car was waiting on the corner of the crowded streets of Queens Boulevard and 44th Street. It was now 9:45. DeVenuta was driving. Willie said to take it nice and easy to avoid suspicion. They headed over the Queensboro Bridge. As they were headed towards Manhattan, police cars were going by in the other direction with their sirens blasting.

In Manhattan, they went up York Avenue to the East River. Willie took the plates off the car and stuck them in the money sack. Later he hammered them into small squares and dumped them over the side of the Staten Island Ferry into the river.

The guys split up and planned to rendezvous at Tommy Kling's house. Every profession has its unwritten rules. One of the unwritten rules of robbery is that the bag of loot cannot be opened until all the parties participating in the robbery are present. After Willie, Kling, and DeVenuta opened the bag and counted the money, the grand total was just under sixty-four thousand dollars.

The disappointment for Willie Sutton wasn't in the small amount of money. It was that the excitement of the robbery was over. Sometimes, the expectation of doing something far exceeds the excitement of actually doing it.

Over his career, Willie Sutton robbed over one hundred banks using disguises and precision planning. He never injured a soul. He pioneered safecracking techniques and studied the human psyche. He also escaped three times from America's most escape-proof prisons—twice from Sing Sing. His final arrest was in 1952. In 1969, when he was sick in prison, a "Free Willie Sutton" campaign got him freed for a final time.

Willie's famous quote, "That's where the money is," in answer to the question "Why rob banks?" was actually never said by him but instead by a reporter who needed to fill copy space. The quote stuck with him, however, and later became known in medical journals as "Sutton's Law," which is the concept of looking for the obvious before going deeper when diagnosing a patient.

Dead Vaccine
Saves Lives
· 1952 ·

During the 1940s and 1950s, a horrible disease called polio-myelitis was afflicting children and terrifying parents throughout America and the world. There was seemingly no defense against this rampant menace which left its young victims disabled, paralyzed, or worse . . . dead.

Polio, as the disease was commonly known, was caused by a virus. The anxiety among American parents grew to near-hysteria as the affliction claimed more and more victims. Since so many families were suffering from the same fate, local newspapers ran patient lists, noting the age, hometown, and severity of the sickness of each patient. Photographs were published showing children on crutches, in leg braces, and in iron lungs. New

Yorkers were panic-stricken, and many bolted their doors and kept their windows tightly sealed in an attempt to keep out the dreaded infection.

Others, thinking this wasn't enough of a safety measure, fled to the suburbs and unknowingly spread the disease further. Since little was known about the disease, many thought that polio entered the body through the nostrils and then infected the brain. Some people tried to protect themselves by placing zinc-plating on their noses.

While all of this was going on, an unknown doctor named Jonas Salk, who was born in New York City, was desperately trying to develop a vaccine which would immunize people against the dreaded polio virus. The process was a long and difficult undertaking which began with Salk's entry into the medical school at New York University. He decided to specialize in a science called microbiology, the study of microscopic life.

Salk spent a year researching the influenza virus—the virus that causes the flu—and was working on a way to deprive the virus of its ability to infect people. His success in this area prompted him to move forward with a vaccine for polio. He spent eight years working on it.

One of the driving influences on Salk was that he was taught that in order for a person to become immune to a virus, that person must first be infected. He was determined to prove that this was not necessarily so and people could be protected without actually getting the disease.

A big break for Salk came in 1949 when another scientist found a way to grow the polio virus in a test tube. Salk then took samples of the virus and killed and sterilized them. Based on the results he'd seen under his microscope, he believed that when he injected this dead virus into a person, his or her immune system would build up anitbodies which would allow the body to fight off the deadly virus if it was caught from someone else. By 1952, Salk was ready to try his vaccine on people. When Salk saw that his vaccine protected people from getting polio and actually helped cure people who already had it, he was overjoyed.

This discovery was nothing short of a miracle. But the discovery was only the beginning. The nation's worst polio epidemic occurred in 1952. Mass trials with the vaccine were held in 1953. Boldly, in a gesture showing Salk's confidence in his discovery, Salk, his wife, and their sons were among the first to receive the vaccine. For roughly the next two years, as Salk continued his research, more than 1.8 million school children— nicknamed "Polio Pioneers"—participated in a nationwide test of Salk's polio vaccine. It was the largest medical experiment in history.

The trials proved that the polio vaccine was effective. The news of the discovery was made public on April 12, 1955. Jonas Salk instantly became a household name and a world-famous figure. He appeared on the front of newspapers and magazines and was hailed as a miracle worker. He refused to patent the vaccine saying he had no interest in personally profiting from his discovery. He simply wanted the vaccine distributed freely and as widely as possible in order to help the most people. The public was relieved that the horrible disease could now be prevented forever.

There were some reservations about Salk's work. His original vaccine consisted of the "killed" polio virus, but a few years later a vaccine was developed using live polio which could be taken by people orally. Some scientists believed there was evidence that Salk's vaccine did not always completely immunize. Some public health authorities chose to distribute the "live" vaccine instead of Salk's vaccine. The move backfired. The live virus infected some people with the disease.

Salk, who eventually founded the Salk Institute for Biological Studies, was awarded the Presidential Medal of Freedom. Because of his polio vaccine, said author Jane S. Smith, "a generation learned to view health as a birthright, assuming that doctors could provide a cure for any ailment if it were attacked with enough boldness and enough money."

At a time when the nation was terrified of such a horrible disease, and panic-stricken parents were desperate for a cure, research that began at New York University eliminated the fear of polio. One man's determination, curiosity, and belief helped save the lives of millions.

Niagara Falls is Falling Down
· 1954 ·

Shortly after 8 A.M. on July 28, 1954, a Niagara Falls Park patrolman making his usual inspection rounds noticed a crack at the edge of the escarpment overlooking the falls in Prospect Park. The crack was about forty feet upstream from the towering falls. This was no small crack. It ran back from the edge of the high cliff, then ran parallel to the edge for about two hundred feet. Anticipating trouble, the patrolman told the superintendent of the park about the crack, and the area was blocked with snow fences to stop visitors from venturing onto the escarpment.

Precautions had already been taken at the elevators leading down to the famous *Maid of the Mist* steamboat. Suspicions had been aroused the night before when water poured into the elevator shafts and tumbled to the bottom. Normally, a little water got into the shafts, but this was enough to fill buckets. Crews worked all night to try to stop the flow but couldn't. Like the little boy with his finger in the hole of the dike, they knew they had to act quickly or something would burst. The following morning the patrolman discovered the crack. Even though there was still hope that the problem could be solved, the parks commission personnel didn't want to take a chance. They blocked off the area. Good thing they decided to err on the side of caution.

At 4:50 P.M. the same day, a low, bellowing rumble began. As thousands of spectators watched, pavement crevices began to widen. Then the lawn around Prospect Point started to open like a giant, yawning mouth. Wire and iron fences along the edge of the escarpment were torn from the ground. Then all movement stopped. Everyone waited as a moment in time was frozen. Then, as if they had just stopped to take a breather, things began to move again. The fences fell into the Niagara River gorge, pulling huge chunks of rocks with them. The escarpment itself began to crumble, first slowly, then building up speed and crashing down into the gorge, taking trees and shrubs with it.

Gigantic chunks of rocks, some the size of a small house— forty feet in length and from forty to fifty feet in width— plummeted into the gorge. Following like little puppies on a leash, tremendous slabs of rock and earth snapped off the cliff and fell to the mist-shrouded rocks below.

After ten minutes of destruction, there was silence. An estimated 185,000 tons of rock, dirt, and rubble had crumbled into a 170-foot-deep chasm, taking a triangle section two hundred feet wide and about eighty feet deep off cliffs above Niagara Falls. Prospect Point itself, where a visitor used to be able to stand just a few feet away from the crest of the falls, had been rounded off. The rock slide left a giant V-shaped crevice which forever changed the shape of the flank of American Falls.

Seconds after the fall of Niagara Falls was completed, a giant screen of dust billowed up from the gorge. With the dust came a strong stench of sulfur. An hour after the collapse, chocolate brown silt oozed from the heap of rocks that had fallen into the river.

This was the second major rock slide to occur at Niagara Falls in thirty years. In 1931, ironically almost at the same time of day—5 P.M.—on January 17, a U-shaped hollow was ripped out from the American Falls crestline by a seventy-five-thousand-ton rock slide.

The park superintendent, Keith Hopkins, said that the erosion in a stratum of shale apparently caused the rock falls. He explained that the waters rumble over a sixty-foot-thick cap rock which is supported by the shale. After years of being washed by the rumbling water, the shale is eaten away. Once the shale is eaten away there is no support for the cap rock, and pieces of it crumble and fall.

The lip of both the American Falls and Canadian Falls is ninety feet deep and made of limestone, which looks strong, but underneath the lip is Lockport Dolomite and Rochester Shale, followed by sandstone. Basically, this means the falls are built on sand. The pressure of water plunging over the top layer of limestone damages the softer layers below it, causing the falls to recede about five feet per year. Leading experts believe that twenty-five thousand years ago the falls stood at the shores of Lake Ontario.

Immediately after the rock slide of 1954, workmen built a sloping ramp made of native stones and concrete, similar to old cobblestone streets, to fill in the place where Prospect Point was formerly located. This concrete ramp also serves another purpose. It prevents water from seeping through the rocks and further damaging that area.

To preserve the beauty of the falls, remedial efforts were launched in 1954 under the U.S.–Canada Treaty of 1950, which obligates both countries to maintain the beauty of the area. Work was done around the Canadian Falls to distribute the flow of the water so that the rate of erosion at the center of the larger falls would slow down. Underground conduits that run from the falls three and a half miles to the largest hydro electric power system in the world were built. Every night from 9 P.M. to 9 A.M. fifty percent of the water is diverted into the power plant to fill the reservoir. During the day, from 9 A.M. to 9 P.M., the conduit faucet runs full blast as the falls work at full tilt, with 200,000 cubic feet of water flowing per second.

But this still hasn't completely solved the erosion problem. As far as geologists are concerned, if nature takes its course, the picturesque precipice, New York's second largest attraction, will eventually become nothing but a series of rapids.

In 1969 the American Falls were "dewatered." In other words, the falls were shut off. On June 9, 1969, the U.S. Army built a cofferdam extending from the U.S. mainland to Goat Island. When this dangerous four-day undertaking was accomplished, geologists studied the exposed rocks to determine what measures could be taken to prevent future rock slides.

Tourists were allowed to walk on the dried-up rock bed. As *Niagara Gazette* reporter Don Glynn said, "The dried up channel reeked with slimy seaweeds and broken limbs from low-hanging shrubbery and trees upriver." Twelve quarts of coins tossed over the centuries were recovered, as well as two dead bodies. Four days later, on June 13, 1969, the falls were restored.

The Stolen Star
·1964·

The 563-carat Star of India is one of the world's most famous rocks. It was donated to the American Museum of Natural History by its former owner, millionaire legend J.P. Morgan. Unlike the cursed Hope Diamond, the Star of India was said to bring joyful good fortune to all its owners. According to legend, star stones were part of the Star of Bethlehem, and their glowing rays represented hope, faith, and destiny.

Maybe it was the allure of this good fortune that convinced two bronzed-bodied, golden-haired Miami surf bums, twenty-seven-year-old Jack Murphy, nicknamed "Murf the Surf," and his buddy, twenty-six-year-old Allan Dale Kuhn, to commit one of the greatest criminal gem capers in history.

Shortly after watching Jules Dassin's film *Topkapi*, a movie detailing a gem theft from an Istanbul museum, these two professional aquatic acrobats decided to relieve the Museum of Natural History of $410,000 worth of gems on October 30th, 1964.

These two dubious characters were already under surveillance by the Miami Police Department. With their Cadillacs, yachts, and bevy of babes, they were living high above any visible means of support. But this didn't stop them from keeping a low profile.

Roger Frederick Clark, a Meriden, Connecticut, resident and the lookout guy in this caper, worked in Miami for two years. At the end of September 1964, he came back to New York and stayed with his mom for about five weeks. Then, on October 6, he rented a swank suite in the Cambridge House Hotel on West 86th Street, which became the headquarters for the gem operation.

A week after the apartment was rented, Kuhn and Murphy drove up from Florida in a '64 convertible with two stunning women. The two surfers seemingly developed a love for the Museum of Natural History and made frequent trips to Central Park West and 77th Street to familiarize themselves with the museum grounds.

At 8 P.M. on that fateful Thursday night in October, Murphy and Kuhn entered the museum through the 81st Street entrance, leaving Clark outside as the lookout. All three communicated through walkie-talkies. Being acrobats, they easily scaled a ten-foot wall at the back of the museum, forced a lock on the ground floor, then walked up the stairs to the fifth floor where the offices of personnel, laboratories, and other facilities not open to the public were located.

Having done their homework, they knew the layout of the building, and they went directly to Room 38, which is situated above the J.P. Morgan Hall of Gems and Minerals Gallery.

From Room 38, Murphy and Kuhn observed the movements of the eight museum guards responsible for the twenty-three acres of the Museum of Natural History. When the moment was right, they made their daring descent.

A work table was positioned by Room 38's fifth floor window. They climbed onto the table, out the window, and using the strong nylon tape of a venetian blind, lowered themselves to the gem gallery fifteen feet below and got into the gallery through an unlocked window. They had to work carefully since they were above a one-hundred-foot drop to the cement ground below.

They entered the impressive gallery with its high arched ceilings and hundreds of glass cases. They had their eyes fixed on the two center cases which held the prize collections. After using a glass cutter and a heavy squeegee to break into the cases, they were like kids in a donut shop. They helped themselves to an assortment of gems: the Star of India, the largest cut sapphire known to man, weighing in at 563.35 carats, bigger than a golf ball; the Midnight Star, a dark purple gem at 116.75 carats; the 100.32 Karat DeLong ruby, considered the world's most perfect gem of its class; two engraved emeralds valued at twenty-two thousand dollars; two aquamarines; uncut diamonds and several diamond bracelets, brooches and rings. In all, they stole twenty-four gems. They exited out the window from which they had entered.

For Murphy and Kuhn it was an easy take. Why? Because embarrassingly enough, the Museum of Natural History's priceless world treasures were guarded by an elaborate burglar alarm system that hadn't worked for several years! As if that wasn't bad enough, none of the gems was insured.

At 9:15 the next morning, Murphy and Kuhn flew back to Miami, and Clark went to his mom's house in Connecticut. The police were right on the case. The crime scene in the museum was blocked off. Somehow they obtained a pair of sneakers about size eight which matched the sole marks on the table near the fifth floor window. They started showing around pictures of suspects, including Murphy and Kuhn. Employees of some west side hotels made positive identifications and during the afternoon after the heist, the Cambridge House hotel suite was seized with a search warrant. In the suite they found burglary tools, a blackjack, photographs of the roof and interior of the museum, a book called the "Story of Gems," and heroin and marijuana.

How the police found the apartment so quickly is a mystery. Some people believe the police obtained information from a fence that the two were connected with. Others say Murphy and Kuhn were tracked through fingerprints on the gem cases. Police kept their sources confidential.

Either way, by 2:30 A.M. on October 31, six New York City policemen and two FBI men arrested Clark and a friend of his when they showed up at the Cambridge suite. Clark was booked on charges of burglary, possession of burglary tools, possession of a blackjack, possession of narcotics, possession of marijuana, and violation of the Sullivan Law (having possession of a gun with two expended shells). Shortly after, Murphy and Kuhn were arrested in Florida.

Unfortunately for police, there wasn't enough evidence to pin the crime on them. Free on bond, they became overnight celebrities in the criminal world. They joked about opening a night spot called The Star of India, where waitresses would wear saris.

They looked as if they had gotten off scot-free until actress Eva Gabor stepped in. She spotted their pictures in a paper and decided that they were the guys who had pistol-whipped her and taken her bracelet a year earlier. She filed a complaint.

Facing this fresh charge, Kuhn, in January of 1965, cut a deal with the Manhattan District Attorney, Frank Hogan, saying he might be able to locate the gems for an exchange of "consider ations." The uninsured museum was thrilled. Eventually, at the end of a long trail that ended in a bus station locker, inside a bag, the Star of India and a few other gems were recovered.

Eva Gabor never followed through on the burglary charge. The two surf bums who had lifted one of the most famous gems of all time served only two years on simple burglary charges. Clark served time on the Sullivan Law violation. When they were released, all three enjoyed fame as the classy gentlemen behind one of the world's most famous capers.

In 1968, Jack "Murf the Surf" Murphy reentered prison and served twenty-one years, charged with the murders of two young women who were found beaten to death and tied to concrete blocks and then dumped into a Florida canal. After he got out of prison he wrote an award-winning book, *Jewels for the Journey.* He is presently the regional director of Bill Glass Ministries and can be seen on many Christian radio and TV shows.

London Beatles Invade Shea Stadium
· 1965 ·

When the Beatles left the London airport on August 13, 1965, as one thousand screaming, adoring fans gave them a send-off worthy of British royalty, they were actually preparing to make rock 'n' roll history when they arrived in New York City. The Beatles were ready to perform at Shea Stadium in Flushing, Queens before 55,600 jubilant fans—a world record audience.

The concert was such a hugely anticipated happening that it was going to be filmed for a later television special. The Beatles were the most popular band of their time. Thousands were waiting for this great event. An aura of madness was expected to overtake Shea Stadium.

Since they burst onto the scene in 1962 in Liverpool, England, the Beatles—John Lennon, Paul McCartney, George Harrison, and Ringo Starr—had quickly become world famous. They became part of what was known as the "British Invasion," where England's most popular rock 'n' roll bands were hitting the American airwaves and giving live concerts.

The Beatles had performed in the United States for the first time during an American tour in 1964. They played around the country to relatively small audiences. Their most famous appearance was on the Ed Sullivan Show which aired live. They were a huge success. By the time the Shea Stadium concert was booked,

America was very familiar with the Beatles, and they already had a huge following among American music fans.

The Shea Stadium concert, which would be the Beatles's first on a month-long American tour, actually provoked outrageous reactions from fans two days before the concert took place. As the band geared up for the big event, they taped a session at the CBS studios in midtown Manhattan which would be aired on the Ed Sullivan Show on September 12. More than one thousand fanatical followers tried to crash the afternoon rehearsal and the dress rehearsal and the actual taping at night.

Soon after the Beatles arrived at the studio from the Warwick Hotel, teenagers shrieked wildly outside, creating a situation that bordered on bedlam. While the band rehearsed and then taped six songs that day, police needed to set up wooden barricades outside the studio. Pandemonium broke loose as the police battled Beatles worshippers who were dying to get close to their idols. Police officers were forced to run from one trouble spot to another in their attempts to keep the unruly crowd in some kind of order.

Inside the studio, the Beatles went about their business, blasting their loud electric guitars, an electric organ, and Ringo's drums. When they took a break as the set was being changed, the shrill and piercing sounds of the fans could be heard in the studio. Waves of cries would ebb and flow especially when a side door was opened briefly. The Beatles just considered this normal New York behavior.

Even the police got caught up in the excitement over the Beatles invasion. While they battled fans outside, many officers in the studio approached the Beatles, pen and paper in hand, asking for autographs. A common refrain was, "If I don't get an autograph, my daughter will . . ." The "Fab Four" were very understanding and generous. They signed for the cops gladly.

When the rehearsal ended shortly before 2 P.M., the seven hundred fans who actually had tickets for the dress rehearsal pushed forward on the barricades, screamed and shouted triumphantly, and went inside when the doors finally opened. Two girls were caught with bogus tickets and wept uncontrollably as they were ushered out.

By this time, another line was growing along 54th Street for the taping session. Some fans in this line had arrived as early as 6 A.M. Ed Sullivan had a terse comment on the day's events. "It's murder," he said.

The next day, as the hour of the Shea Stadium concert approached, the actions of the fans became as big a story as the music and the Beatles themselves. The concert gathering was the largest collection of rock fans ever assembled in one place. Although the show was supposed to begin at 8 P.M., the Beatles did not arrive until 9:17 P.M. in an armored car that was kept running throughout the duration of the band's performance in case the Beatles needed a quick escape.

The crowd, impatient until the Beatles's arrival, broke into hysteria when they finally arrived. Fans wept, stamped their feet, and some even fainted. The crowd was so loud and boisterous that fans couldn't even hear the music. But they didn't care. All that mattered was that they were watching their idols in person.

As the Beatles performed near second base on the baseball field, some of the fans near the front row begged police to bring them blades of grass, simply because the Beatles had walked on them. One policewoman remarked, "They are psychos. Their mothers ought to see them now." During the thirty minutes that the band performed, police watched the crowd carefully as hundreds of flashbulbs went off and young girls sobbed the Beatles's first names. Many girls who had fainted or were in hysterics were carried to the first-aid dressing room on the stadium's ground level.

The Beatles, used to adoring crowds, were still affected by the enormous size of this one. They got caught up in all the excitement. They strummed their guitars and tapped their feet with great enthusiasm and waved to the crowd. John Lennon began playing the organ with his elbow. Although fifty amplifiers had been set up on the field, the singing was drowned out by the piercing noise of the fans.

Thirteen television cameras—including one in a helicopter—taped the incredible event for Ed Sullivan Productions. When the Beatles finally finished their performance, they were rushed off the stage and into the same vehicle that had driven them to the stadium. The fans continued to go berserk, many crying that the concert was over and others simply sobbing because they loved the band.

For more than an hour after the concert ended, police still had their hands full with concert-goers who needed to be rounded up in the stands and carried off the field.

The Beatles made about $160,000 from this sold-out performance. To their fans who paid for the privilege of seeing them, it was worth every penny. The concert at Shea Stadium was the first of its kind anywhere in the world. It was an event people would always remember, not just as a rock concert, but as a mania that still lingers on in the hearts of many.

Woodstock:
It Started as a Sitcom Idea
• 1969 •

Fifty miles from the town of Woodstock, New York, on a six-hundred-acre dairy farm in the quiet town of Bethel, New York, the muddy pasture of Max Yasgur was the site of one of the biggest counter-cultural events of all time, when 450,000 people created a mini-nation. Woodstock, which has become an instant adjective for hedonism and sixties "flower power," was more than just a concert. It was the ultimate bash, costing more than $2.4 million.

Not wanting to miss out on the fun, people poured in from all over the country, closing the New York State Thruway and creating one of the nation's worst traffic jams ever. Nothing could stop it—the event took on a life of its own and no one was prepared for this horde of party-goers. Nothing like this had ever happened in the history of music.

It started innocently enough when two creative young men wanted to write a sitcom as a way to become famous. After John Roberts, a twenty-six-year-old heir to a multimillion-dollar trust fund, who had only seen one concert in his life, and twenty-four-year-old Joel Rosenman, a guitar-playing lounge act and Yale Law School graduate, met on a golf course, they eventually roomed together and decided to write a male version of *I Love Lucy*. The plot was to be based on "two pals with more money than brains and a thirst for adventure" who every week would find another get-rich-quick scheme to invest in. To get ideas for episodes, they took out an ad in the *New York Times* in March 1968, as if they were looking for real business ventures. As the ideas poured in, they decided to actually use one of the suggestions.

Enter now the other two key players: Artie Kornfeld, age twenty-five, the vice president of Capitol Records who had written thirty hit singles, and Michael Lang, who owned the first drug paraphernalia shop in the state of Florida and had produced one of the biggest rock shows ever—the two-day Miami Pop Festival.

When Lang and Kornfeld met, they hit it off and soon became roommates. They came up with the idea to organize a festival for the purpose of raising money to open a state-of-the-art recording studio in Woodstock, New York. Ulster County was chosen because top musicians such as Bob Dylan, Van Morrison, Jimi Hendrix, and Janis Joplin were moving to the area.

Kornfeld and Lang approached Roberts and Rosenman with the proposal. They planned to host the world's biggest rock 'n' roll show with a budget of $500,000. The four formed a corporation called Woodstock Ventures Inc. The extravaganza was now a calculated commercial venture set in motion.

In early April, they found a site for ten thousand dollars in Wallkill, New York: the three-hundred-acre Mills Industrial Park. The concert was set for August. But when the town's residents heard about the planned event, they started getting nervous about the potential massive attendance and the "hippie freaks" that would overtake their town.

Meanwhile, Ventures Inc. was cultivating a cool public relations image by putting ads in underground newspapers like *The Village Voice* and *Rolling Stone*. By May, ads began running in the *New York Times*. The slogan, "Three Days of Peace and Music," and the famous symbol of the dove on the guitar were gaining notoriety.

The foursome now had to find artists to perform at the event. But the top musicians of the day were reluctant to sign, since Ventures Inc. was unknown. Rosenman decided to offer double what the psychedelic bands of the era were normally paid.

Jefferson Airplane was paid an unprecedented twelve thousand dollars to perform. Other groups then fell in line. In all, $180,000 was spent on talent. While the promoters created an image of free love and music, Woodstock was never intended to be a charity event.

Next, they recruited the only local sound system engineer, Allan Markoff, to build the sound system. According to Markoff, it was "tantamount to doing a sound system for thirty million people today." At their lowest volume setting, the Woodstock speakers would cause pain for anyone standing within ten feet.

The Wallkill townspeople were now in an uproar. They were threatening to blow up the house of Howard Mills, the owner of land where the concert was to be held if he let the concert go on. The townspeople passed a law forbidding gatherings of more than five thousand people; the law was meant to shut down Woodstock. With one month left to go, Ventures Inc. had to find a new concert site. Advanced ticket sales were already at 180,000.

The promoters finally hooked up with Max Yasgur, a milk and cheese farmer. They met in his alfalfa field and immediately knew the field was the place for the concert. "It was magic," Lang said. The deal was set for a price of seventy-five thousand dollars.

New concerns arose about the potential drug, traffic, and sewage problems that could arise. The people who lived in the area protested at Yasgur's farm. To soothe fears, Ventures Inc. delved in creative deception by saying only fifty thousand people would show, although they actually thought a quarter of a million people would come.

Two days before the concert, Kornfeld convinced Warner Brothers to donate one hundred thousand dollars to film the event. Martin Scorsese agreed to direct the production. It was a crap shoot—either the best concert ever or a riot of unprecedented proportions would be captured on film.

Twenty-four hours before the concert, Ventures Inc. knew it would have major problems. It did. Traffic was jammed for ten miles; food trucks couldn't get through; the performers had to be flown in by helicopters; no ticket booths could be set up; the fence separating the people who had prepaid from the incoming masses came down, and Woodstock became a free concert from that point on.

Police officers refused to get involved for fear of losing their jobs—side work was not sanctioned. Members of a hippie commune known as the "The Hog Farmers" were bussed in to act as security and build makeshift kitchens and tents for the masses.

The concert was supposed to start at 4 P.M. on Friday, August 15. The first performers were supposed to be folk singers. But because of mass confusion, traffic jams, and growing tension in the crowd, it was not until 5:07 P.M. that the organizers enlisted the first performer who was ready, Richie Havens, to perform. He played on for more than three hours, improvising songs until musical reinforcements came to the rescue. The concert was saved by U.S. Army helicopters, which was ironic since many in the crowd were anti-war. The helicopters brought in the musicians so they could perform.

To keep the crowd from getting restless, Country Joe McDonald was thrown on stage and came out yelling, "Give me an F," reviving the crowd with anti-war cheers. The improvised song that resulted became known as the Fish Cheer. Sly and the Family Stone had the place rocking with the song, "I Want to Take You Higher."

It started to rain on Friday at midnight while Ravi Shankar was playing. By the time Joan Baez finished singing "We Shall Overcome," a thunderstorm had attacked the Woodstock Nation, as the gathering had come to be called. Within three hours, five inches of rain fell, drenching tents, sleeping bags, and people, and creating a massive, slippery, mud-filled mess.

Despite the rain, by Saturday morning 250,000 people were gathered, the largest audience in musical history. There was no food left. Helicopters had to fly food in. A human chain of two hundred people had to form a circle to clear a space for the helicopters to land. A tractor trailer used to haul away the sewage from portable toilets accidentally ran over a seventeen-year-old boy tucked in his sleeping bag, killing him.

Medical "freak out" tents were set up with three divisions: to deal with hundreds of people hallucinating; to tend to people with feet cut to ribbons from broken glass; and to help those suffering from burned eyes from staring up at the sun. Ventures Inc. asked the government in Albany to have a state of emergency declared but the request was denied.

The organizers were trying to deal with things. They got local groups to make thousands of sandwiches and tried to convince the performers to play twice as long. Janis Joplin, The Who, and the Grateful Dead refused to play unless they were paid up front. The Sullivan County National Bank provided an emergency loan of $100,000 to pay them.

That night it hailed. The Grateful Dead band members were standing in water with their electric guitars, shocking their fingers as they played. People were now receiving emergency medical treatment for heatstroke and pneumonia caused by being drenched for two days.

By Sunday, 450,000 people were in attendance, although one estimate based on aerial photos had the figure at 700,000. The final performers were The Band, Joe Cocker, Crosby Stills and Nash, Ten Years After, Johnny Winter, and Jimi Hendrix, who was brought in late under the condition that he be paid thirty-two thousand dollars to be the final performer. Hendrix concluded the concert with his guitar solo based on the "Star Spangled Banner," which was said to have been the most memorable event of Woodstock.

Woodstock grew far beyond the concert Ventures Inc. planned. Pandemonium ensued. Thousands were injured or became sick, three people died, and several babies were born. At the same time, Woodstock, with its free love, drugs, and the greatest lineup of rock musicians ever assembled was one hell of a party!

A Tight Walk
Between Two Towers
· 1974 ·

Hundreds of spectators stared 1,350 feet up into the gray, early morning sky and shouted cheers of encouragement to a tiny black-clad figure on a cable strung between the Twin Towers. This daring Evel Knieval-type with the grace and dexterity of an acrobat was twenty-five year-old French high-wire artist Philippe Petit.

At 7:15 A.M. on August 7, 1974, Petit sprang into action, leaping past the guards at the World Trade Center and onto the 131-foot, tightly-strung cable wire that he and his friends had set up the night before. He grabbed his balancing pole and for forty-five minutes the thin, blond Petit, wearing black ballet shoes, tiptoed, twirled and did deep knee bends and other stunts with balancing pole in hand that delighted the audience of construction workers, office workers and even policemen below. He waved to his fans and was in sheer heaven. "I couldn't help laughing—it was so beautiful," he later said.

Petit said the urge to walk between the towers just overtook him. Like the man who sees a mountain and has to climb it, he saw the towers and knew he had to try his tightrope stunt. It was in his blood, he said.

Petit's high-wire show ended when a Port Authority of New York and New Jersey police officer shouted, "Get off there or I'll come out and we'll both go down." Petit jumped off the wire into the building and shouted "Bon!" He was immediately handcuffed and led out of the building.

As Petit was directed to the waiting police car, spectators booed the policeman for ending their show. Construction workers tried to shake hands with Petit even though he was in handcuffs. He was taken to Beekman Hospital, examined, and fed. After he was examined and found to be in great shape, he was booked for disorderly conduct and criminal trespass at the Ericsson Place station house and kept for several hours in the Men's House of Detention while he waited for his arraignment.

Petit had been planning this stunt for three months. He had made over two hundred trips to the World Trade Center to plot this aerial performance. He had pulled off two other similar stunts in the past—one between the towers of the Sydney Harbor Bridge in Australia in 1973 and the other at the spires of Notre Dame in Paris in 1971. Petit was a pro at this. He earned his living as a street artist doing pantomime and acrobatic acts. Performing stunts was what thrilled him. He claims he did them for a thrill, not to gain publicity or for money.

After he studied every aspect of the Twin Towers, Petit was ready to put his plan into action. Three days before the big event, he and four other friends, disguised as hard hat construction workers, took a cable, some rope, guy lines, and other equipment to the top floors of the North Tower. The tower was still under construction at the time. Because Petit and his friends were dressed as construction workers, no one questioned them. They used the freight elevator and hid their equipment near the roof. Then two of the accomplices moved from the North to the South Tower.

They waited until nightfall. Still undetected, they set up shop on the North Tower roof. They used a five-foot crossbow and arrow to project the cable to the South Tower. With a line established, they passed the heavier lines back and forth until they could lay a galvanized steel cable on top of the other wires. One end of the cable was tightly wound around a stationary steel stanchion that was located on the roof. The other end was hooked up to a winch which could adjust the tension of the rope as needed. Once the main cable was in place, lines were secured from the roof to hold the main line and minimize swaying. The only unknown factor was how strongly and from what direction the wind was going to kick in. The wind at that height was pretty stiff.

Petit, a native of Nemours, France, said he loved the idea that New Yorkers would wake up and discover a high-wire walker at the Twin Towers. Petit had no fear—he had done this many times before and to him it was a "precise thing." As he described it, "dying of happiness."

His good will must have spread to the authorities, because after Petit had spent a few hours in jail, Manhattan District Attorney Richard H. Kuh held a press conference at the criminal court building and announced the impending dismissal of charges. He agreed to release Petit under one condition—he must promise to do a free aerial performance in a city park "for the children of the city" in exchange for dropping the charges. Petit happily agreed.

Mr. Kuh later acknowledged that the security at the World Trade Center wasn't as "keen" as it should be. Petit's friends, not wanting to miss out on the action, went around to newspaper offices offering to sell exclusive up-close pictures taken from the roof of one of the towers of Petit in action.

As Petit left the detention center, fans surrounded him, trying to get his autograph. One police officer drew two towers on a napkin and asked Petit to sign the napkin. Flashbulbs sparkled and reporters eagerly surrounded him and asked him questions.

"Why did you do it Mr. Petit?"

"When I see two towers I just want to put my wire across. Bon!" he responded.

"What are your future dreams, Mr. Petit?" The high-wire artist paused and thought for a moment. In a spurt of enthusiasm he announced, "I would like to cross Niagara Falls . . . but who knows? For that I need permission." He exited the press conference victorious, having stirred excitement in one of the greatest cities of the world.

The Amityville Horror
·1975·

On the warm night of November 13, 1974, in the town of Amityville, Long Island, Ronald DeFeo, Jr. gruesomely murdered his entire family. He went from room to room and methodically shot his parents, two brothers, and two sisters while they slept. DeFeo, twenty-three years old, had a history of criminality and drug and alcohol abuse. This brutal crime, committed at number 112 on Ocean Avenue, a quiet tree-lined suburban street with well-kept homes and manicured lawns, became one of the most notorious mass murders in Long Island history.

As stunned neighbors and reporters stood by the next evening watching, the victims were removed in body bags. The crowd gasped in horror as a dead child's body fell from its body bag onto the cold pavement. It was picked up and placed in the coroner's van.

At first, DeFeo claimed to have discovered the bodies of his family after arriving home. The night of the murder, Ronald DeFeo Jr. had run into a local bar screaming that his family had been murdered. With three friends, he went back to his home. The four men viewed DeFeo's parents lying dead in their bed. Ronald DeFeo, Sr. was shot in the center of his back. Mrs. DeFeo's wound could not be seen, as she was covered with blankets. Across the hall, DeFeo's two little brothers, aged nine and eleven, one in his pajamas and one in shorts, were both found shot and covered with blood. DeFeo's two sisters, aged thirteen and eighteen, also lay shot dead in their beds. One neighbor told a reporter that she heard the DeFeo's dog howling at about 3:15 A.M. on the night of the crime, which was then assumed to be the approximate hour of the brutal killings.

Two days later, DeFeo confessed to police that he had murdered his family as they slept because he would be the sole beneficiary of a $200,000 insurance policy. Police reported that DeFeo used a rifle which he later dumped in a New York City sewer. Newspapers described DeFeo as "remorseless."

About a year passed quietly, with the DeFeo house vacant, as Ronald Defeo eventually went to trial. Almost a year to the day after the murders—on November 21, 1975—Ronald DeFeo was convicted of second degree murder of all six of his family members. Two weeks later he was sentenced to six consecutive twenty-five-year-to-life prison terms. The judge called the killings the "most heinous and abhorrent crimes."

While the details of these ghastly murders added up to a gruesomely spectacular crime, it was actually the events that were to shortly follow that would forever become known as the "Amityville Horror."

Days after DeFeo was convicted—on December 18, 1975—George and Kathy Lutz, with their three young children, moved into the DeFeo house, saying that the fact that the murders took place there didn't bother them. Twenty-eight days later, they ran from the house claiming it was haunted by demons. They told stories of evil spirits and strange occurrences which took place during their short stay in the house. What the Lutzes claimed to have encountered in that house became international news, with countless television and radio appearances, a best-selling book (with several sequels) and a hit Hollywood movie, all bearing the title, *The Amityville Horror*. The subtitle of the book was *A True Story*.

What the Lutzes claimed happened in the twenty-eight days they lived in the house would terrify even the bravest soul. According to the Lutzes, strange psychic phenomena took over the house in the form of evil spirits which gave George the urge to kill his family. He says he would constantly awaken at 3:15 A.M., the alleged time of the DeFeo murders. George also heard loud marching bands in the house. The heat would turn off for no reason. A black substance would appear in the toilet and the house would be filled with awful smells. George would beat his children for no reason, and he would actually see Ronald DeFeo's face in the "red room" in the basement.

The Lutzes also claimed that hundreds of flies would appear out of nowhere. They said that a local priest, who came to bless the house, was overtaken by a strange illness in the house and nearly crashed on the highway on his way home. The same priest then developed the stigmata (bleeding wounds on his hands similar to the wounds Jesus suffered). George saw a "demon pig" which identified itself as "Jodie," staring with red eyes through the window from outside. The Lutzes also said they saw the image of a demon burning in the fireplace. In one horrifying episode, George saw Kathy levitate two feet off her bed! In another instance, Kathy turned into a ninety-year-old woman before George's eyes.

After the Lutzes came forward with their story, the public also learned that a ceramic lion in the house bit George, the house's wooden door was ripped mysteriously from its hinges, green slime oozed out of the walls, and a deep voice warned the family, "Get out!"

As the Lutzes toured the country with their story, the Amityville Horror became part of the American landscape. Visitors drove from all over just to get a glimpse of the "haunted house." Hordes of people, including ghost hunters, skeptics, drunken teenagers, and the just plain curious, all wanted to get a glimpse of what the hysteria was all about. The book based on the stories of the Lutz family, which continued to advertise itself as a true story, became a best seller. The interest in the house increased. Turnout on Ocean Avenue was especially high at Halloween. When a movie based on the event came out in 1979 with James Brolin and Margot Kidder (as George and Kathy Lutz), it billed itself as "based on the book," and the furor over the case grew even stronger.

While all of this was going on, Dr. Stephen Kaplan, a parapsychologist who founded the Parapsychology Institute of America, was meticulously investigating the case. Dr. Kaplan had become suspicious about the case when George Lutz first contacted him and asked him to investigate the house. When Dr. Kaplan informed George that he would be willing to do so but would also go public if he discovered the story to be a hoax, George Lutz abruptly cancelled Dr. Kaplan's investigation.

Sensing the necessity to defend the legitimate field of parapsychology and to protect the public from being duped, Dr. Kaplan, who himself believed in ghosts and haunted houses, began putting together evidence proving that the Amityville Horror was a hoax.

Dr. Kaplan found big holes in the Lutz's story. There were no witnesses to any of the events which took place in the house except for the Lutz family members. None of the neighbors had ever seen or heard anything unusual. Although these events went on for twenty-eight days, George Lutz only went to the police once. The priest named in the story denied that he ever became ill and said he never had the stigmata.

In the book, a police officer was said to have gone to the house and felt a strange presence. The officer named was never even at the house. The author of the book, Jay Anson, admitted that he didn't know if the story was true but was only writing what the Lutzes told him. George himself later admitted that some "literary license" was taken in the book. He also said that Kathy actually levitated only two inches rather than two feet, as he previously had claimed. The book claimed that a window mysteriously slammed on the hand of the Lutz's son and he was brought to Bushwick Hospital. The hospital had no record of this, and George later claimed that he and his wife bandaged up the boy's hand themselves. Television reporter Marvin Scott, who in the book was said to have come down with a strange illness at the house, threatened to sue over this falsehood.

Dr. Kaplan also found big differences between the hardcover and paperback versions of the book, even though a line in the paperback stated that not one word was changed. But entire events were toned down and some of the more outlandish claims by the Lutzes in the hardcover actually became stories that could be explained through natural things such as wind and a bad heating system in the softcover edition. Some die-hard defenders of the horror story began to attribute the events as being in the Lutz's minds.

As the whole story began to unravel, Dr. Kaplan pressed on, going against the tide of massive publicity which was still promoting the story as true. Dr. Kaplan, through letter writing, public speeches, and talk shows, eventually began to win some influential people over. Finally, the big break came when Ronald DeFeo's lawyer, William Weber, admitted that he and George Lutz had fabricated the story. Weber was trying to secure an insanity defense for DeFeo by showing the house was haunted. The Lutzes were in debt and needed the money DeFeo offered them to play along. In one lawsuit against the Lutzes, a federal judge said the book was "a work of fiction." And no professional parapsychologists ever found anything unusual about the house.

Dr. Kaplan eventually attended a Halloween party at the house at the invitation of the new owners. His final conclusion was "This house is not a horror. This house is a home."

Night of Terror and Looting: Blackout
• 1977 •

O n one of the most unusually hot and humid nights of the summer of 1977, New Yorkers were occupying themselves in the usual way. Baseball fans at Shea Stadium were watching the Mets play the Chicago Cubs. Broadway actors were performing for happy audiences. Patrons relaxed at restaurants and bars. New York City Mayor Abe Beame was giving a campaign speech. And garbage trucks were making their nightly rounds.

And then the lights went out.

At 9:43 P.M. on July 13, lightning struck the Con Edison electrical transmission lines in Westchester County, which supplies the electrical power to New York City, causing all power to turn off.

At first, some people were just confused, thinking the power simply went out in their own homes. Others realized that the problem was bigger than that. Mayor Beame joked to his audience at the Traditional Synagogue in the Bronx, "See . . . this is what you get for not paying your bills."

But eventually, New Yorkers began to realize that the unthinkable had happened. The greatest city in the world was in total darkness. Now, the Broadway actors were performing with the use of flashlights. Surgeons operated under candlelight, and one team of doctors even went to the parking lot to operate using car headlights.

Air conditioners were useless. Subway lights, water pumps, and elevators were all out of service. Thousands of extra police officers were called to duty. The Bronx House of Detention feared a breakout and requested emergency assistance. Gasoline generators were used to light City Hall.

But the biggest story of the Blackout of 1977 was the criminal looting which took place during the hours of darkness, stamping New York as a city gone mad. Before calm—and electricity—were restored twenty-five hours later and the mayor declared the "state of emergency" over, some 3,500 people were arrested, overflowing New York's jails. Just to hold the looters, the city had to reopen the Tombs, a Manhattan jail that had been closed by a federal court order back in 1974 because it was too decrepit to house criminals.

The rampaging began almost immediately, with crowds of people setting hundreds of fires and looting thousands of stores. Roving bands of looters wrenched steel shutters and grills from storefronts with crowbars. Stores with unprotected windows had them shattered. Men, women, and even little children ran off with everything they could carry and destroyed what they could not.

Clothing was taken, as were televisions, jewelry, liquor, food, furniture, and even drugs. A police officer in Bedford-Stuyvesant, Brooklyn, remarked, "It's like a fever struck them. They were out there with trucks, vans, trailers, everything that could roll." Police caught one man with three hundred sink stoppers and another with a case of clothespins.

At Hearn's department store in Brooklyn, kids pulled the clothing from store mannequins, then broke the limbs off the mannequins and threw them on the street. At the Ace Pontiac showroom in the Bronx, looters knocked down a steel door and stole fifty new cars valued at $250,000 by putting the ignition wires together to get the cars started.

On East 14th Street in Manhattan, teenagers snatched the purses of defenseless women. Adults stuffed shopping bags with steaks and roasts stolen from a meat market in Manhattan. At a store nearby, two ten-year-old boys tried to carry away a television set. A woman snatched three radios from the same store.

The police had their hands full. Everywhere they went to scare looters away would only find them running to a different location to stop another set of looters. Some people who weren't looting still helped the criminals by whistling when the cops came by. Looters who were chased away simply went to the next block to take from another store.

Arsonists kept the authorities just as busy as the looters. Firemen fought 1,037 blazes and responded to 1,700 false alarms, which were set to divert attention from the looters, or just for fun. As firemen showed up at the scenes, crowds pelted them with rocks and bottles. At one fire in a Brooklyn store, twenty-two firemen were hurt. In a looted factory warehouse, arsonists set a fire which spread to four tenements and two houses. Altogether, fifty-nine firemen were injured doing their thankless jobs.

In perhaps the most devastated area of the city, Bushwick, Brooklyn, a shopping area with jewelry, clothing, appliance, and furniture stores, was the scene of enterprising criminals who parked rented trucks on the street and filled them with couches, refrigerators, and TV sets. With the police and fire departments so vastly outnumbered, looters simply ran from the scene when they saw police coming, and the fires basically destroyed whatever the looters didn't take.

Streams of black water from broken fire hydrants filled the streets. Twisted steel grilles lay across the sidewalks. In Fedco supermarket, mashed produce, melted ice cream, and broken bottles covered the floor, inches deep. In the South Bronx, fifty-five thousand dollars worth of goods was stolen from R & M Furniture Store. A tipster told police of one looter who had stashed away two thousand dollars worth of furniture in his basement. It got to the point where looters were stealing from other looters.

While many people cheered on the looters, most New Yorkers were outraged. Not only were store owners losing their businesses but people would be out of jobs. One man complained that the looting of one particular drugstore might place his sick mother in danger. Other people who wanted food found there was none left to buy.

In many communities, however, neighbors joined together to protect their property. In Clinton Hill, Brooklyn, homeowners sat on their stoops, passing around cigarettes, candles, and flashlights. Young men armed with baseball bats and iron pipes helped store owners guard their property on a five-block section of Myrtle Avenue. A security guard at an A & P, with four clerks and the manager, brandished a pearl-handled machete to chase away a gang of thirty looters. Many storeowners armed themselves with pistols, rifles, and shotguns and sat up all night by their stores.

With all the chaos, the police were surprisingly restrained. Eight thousand cops were called to duty—twice the number that were supposed to be on duty that night. Because of the experiences from the riots of the 1960s, the police were well-trained in riot control. Some rioters were let go with a warning, but many were arrested. With all the arrests, the city's courthouse holding pens were crammed with ten prisoners in cells designed for one.

Still, the ingenuity and kindness of honest New Yorkers came through. One man wearing a cape and holding a pink flare directed traffic on the corner of 79th Street and Park Avenue in Manhattan. Sixteen people turned Coney Island's 150-foot high Wonder Wheel by hand so that stranded riders could reach the ground. At city hotels, guests who could not reach their rooms were provided with food. At the Empire State Building, visitors who were forced to spend the night on the 86th floor were given free breakfasts.

As the city tried to recover, New Yorkers spent the next few days wondering what could cause such awful behavior during a time of crisis. New York's night of terror saw a loss to the city's businesses and property of around one billion dollars. You never know what can happen when the lights go out.

Miracle On Ice
· 1980 ·

As the 1980 Winter Olympics approached in Lake Placid, New York, international tensions were very high. Americans were being held hostage in Iran by the Ayatollah Khomeini, Soviet troops had invaded Afghanistan, and Americans were angered and frustrated by the fact that Russia was aligned with America's enemy, Iran. Normally, the Olympics symbolized international brotherhood. But in February of 1980, the games meant so much more than simple sports competition—our national pride was at stake.

Although the games usually inspire great suspense and excitement over who the champions will be, there was practically no doubt about who would win the gold medal in Olympic ice hockey. The Russian team was so powerful that it was universally accepted that they were by far the best team in the world. In fact, the Russians had been the dominant team for many years. Their record was so superior to all the other nations that they had been the reigning gold medal champions for sixteen years. And they had not lost a single game since 1968.

There was no reason to think 1980 would be any different. In all the pre-Olympic tournaments, the Russian team made short work of their opponents. One year earlier, the Russians won the Challenge Cup against a team of National Hockey League all-stars. The Russians simply had the best players in the world. If there was to be any sort of competition for the Russians, it would certainly come from the Canadian team or one of the European teams.

The American team was comprised of a bunch of college kids. The team had been formed several months earlier and during the pre-Olympic games had played only average. As the Olympics approached, the American team was improving but was still given relatively no chance of winning a medal against the more established teams.

When the first puck was dropped to start the Olympic hockey competitions, the Americans found themselves in an uphill struggle against Sweden. They still trailed by one goal with less than a minute to play. The American dream of attaining a medal seemed to be going down the drain in the very first game. But the team dramatically tied the game with seconds remaining and the dream remained alive.

The American team seemed to gain momentum from the unlikely tie and went on to shock everyone by winning its next four games. Finally, the medal round arrived and the Americans found themselves in the incredible position of having a chance to not only win a medal, but maybe even the gold. But reality seemed to be staring the team in the face—the mighty Russians were waiting.

While the Americans were writing a Cinderella story with their 4-0-1 record entering the medal round, the powerful Russians had gone about their business as everyone expected. They had five wins and no losses, and there was no reason to think the Russians wouldn't win the next two games and hold onto the gold medal they had owned for the past sixteen years. They had even defeated the Americans just two weeks earlier by a score of 10 to 3 in an exhibition.

But on a cold Friday night in Lake Placid, the USA would finally meet the Soviet team in a game that would forever change the face of American hockey.

Before the game, USA coach Herb Brooks told his team members, "You are born to be a player. You are meant to be a player. This moment is yours, and you are meant to be here. Use poise and possession with the puck."

Still, no one believed the Americans could win—except the players themselves. When the game finally started, the Russians took control and generally outplayed the Americans for the first two periods. But Jim Craig, the American goaltender, was swatting away Russian shots and keeping the Americans in the game. As each team skated up and down the ice with the puck, the crowd at the Olympic Fieldhouse arena cheered wildly, begging the Americans to pull off a miracle.

Thanks to the miraculous play of Craig and the remarkable performances of the other young Americans, the Russians led by only one goal; the score was 3 to 2 in the final period. But time was running out.

Suddenly, with only slightly more than eleven minutes to go in the game, forward Mark Johnson scored for the Americans on a power play (a one-man advantage awarded because of a penalty). Unbelievably, the game was tied. The miracle seemed possible.

Then, with ten minutes left in the game, the captain of the American team, Mark Eruzione, closed in on the Soviet goal with the puck. A defenseman stood between Eruzione and the Russian goal. Eruzione decided to shoot. When the puck went in and the Americans had taken the lead, pandemonium broke out on the ice. Teammates swarmed off the bench and smothered Eruzione on the sideboards. But there was still time left in the game.

Eruzione said, "First, I was real excited. . . . After that, I just kept going around to the guys and telling them to relax. But you know what? I don't think God could have come down and got us to relax."

The final ten minutes of the game seemed like an eternity. The Russians put on so much pressure that the rink seemed to be tilted—the puck always sliding toward the American goal. But the Americans held fast and goaltender Jim Craig was phenomenal, thwarting the Russians on every shot. As the final minute approached, the arena was electric. Desperate to hang on, the Americans kept clearing the puck as the Russians launched one last desperate attempt to tie the game.

When the clock showed only five seconds remaining, sports announcer Al Michaels screamed, "Do you believe in miracles? . . Yes!"

The Americans had done it. As teammates threw their sticks in the air and mobbed Jim Craig, a wild celebration was touched off, the likes of which no one had ever seen before. Not only the players but fans flooded the streets chanting "USA, USA" as fireworks cascaded across the sky.

All across America, a troubled nation found joy in the remarkable accomplishment of their national team. The victory went beyond sports fans to include all Americans who reacted to the triumph as a symbol of national pride. President Jimmy Carter called Coach Brooks and said how proud the team had made the people of the United States. It was as if an amateur club fighter had stepped into the ring with the heavyweight champion of the world—and won.

Two days after their defeat of the Russians, in an anti-climactic finish, the Americans defeated Finland by the score of 4 to 2 to win the gold medal. But the game that will be forever etched in the American memory is the impossible victory over the Russians—the miracle on ice.

Flight 800 Blown Out of the Moriches

• 1996 •

At 8:31 P.M. on Wednesday evening, July 17, 1996, TWA's Boeing 747 Jumbo Jet, Flight 800, enroute from New York's John F. Kennedy International Airport to Paris, France, carrying 230 passengers and crew members, exploded in the sky off the coast of Long Island. There were no survivors.

Flight 800 had landed in New York after flying from Athens, Greece. The plane took off from JFK with no problems, as it had done every day for twenty-seven years. Eleven minutes into the flight, and shortly after a controller at the Boston Air Route Traffic Control Center had directed the Flight 800 pilot to ascend to 15,000 feet from its level of 13,700 feet, reports started pouring in from other pilots.

"We just saw an explosion up ahead of us. . . . It just went down . . . in the water," reported Eastwind Flight 507 at 8:32. "It just blew up in the air, and then we saw two fireballs go down to the water. . . . There seemed to be a light." United Airlines Flight 2 confirmed, "It's still burning down there. . . . there's bright red, and there's smoke coming up. . . fire with smoke coming out of the water."

Coast Guard officials reported the plane was "about ten miles offshore to the south of the village of Center Moriches." The Moriches is a small collection of commercial fishing villages filled with wooden cottages about seventy miles from Manhattan on Southeast Long Island.

The area was soon swarming with Coast Guard personnel, police, firemen, and rescue crews. Six helicopters and a Navy P-3 rescue plane came to the site. The gruesome task of recovering the bodies began. The crash site was visible for miles; the media poured in. The debris floating in the water was still brightly burning for three hours after the plane exploded.

By midnight, eighteen bodies had been recovered. Families waited at JFK's Terminal 5 to see if their loved ones had been aboard the plane.

This horrible tragedy sparked the largest investigation since the Space Shuttle Challenger explosion. A sixteen-month probe, at the cost of twenty million dollars, involved the FBI, the Federal Aviation Administration, the State Department, and the National Transportation Safety Board (NTSB). Independent investigations were also conducted by other local and state enforcement agencies, as well as other groups and dedicated individuals.

There were 244 eyewitnesses to the crash who claimed to have seen a missile-like object or streak of light outside the plane immediately before the explosion, giving rise to several theories as to what may have caused the fatal incident.

While the official government investigation was proceeding, other theories and scenarios were put forth from different quarters. One idea was that a bomb placed by terrorists caused the explosion, since Athens, Flight 800's previous departure point, is well known as a base for terrorists. Others felt that since many French citizens were onboard and the United States and France were leaning on Syria to revive talks with the Israelis, Syria carried out a terrorist act.

Lloyd L. Mielke, a retired TWA structural engineer with thirty-nine years experience, believed there was sufficient data to prove a meteor brought down Flight 800. Approximately three thousand substantial-sized meteors hit the earth each month, he said, often hitting cars, dogs, mailboxes, and people. On July 17, a bolide (fragment of a meteor) was recorded at an altitude of nine miles, or around six miles above and ten miles southwest of the where the plane was when it exploded. Fragments of the bolide could have hit the aircraft, explaining the streaks of light witnessed and the sonic boom heard.

Pierre Salinger, who served as an ABC news correspondent from 1978 to 1993 and before that as a press spokesman for President John F. Kennedy, claimed to have possession of a document that proved that a United States Navy missile out of Area W-105 accidentally hit the plane. Salinger explained, "W-105 is a warning area on the southeast coast of Long Island and is used by the military for missile firing and other military operations." These military exercises happen between four and six times per year.

Salinger theorized that a guided-missile-bearing ship fired the missile that brought down the Boeing 747. The strike was accidental due to misinformation received by the ships crew. "These people who are doing these missile tests had been told that airplanes flying in that area would be all flying over 21,000 feet. The fact is that TWA Flight 800 was restricted to 13,000 feet because above it was USAir flight at 21,000 [feet], which was coming down towards Providence, R.I." The ship fired the missile from Norfolk, Virginia, thinking it was safe.

An admiral in the United States Navy was the first person the authorities called after Flight 800 went down. Naval exercises were taking place on that night. The Navy uses the flight path of airplanes leaving New York City airports to "lock on their missile guidance systems" to civilian aircraft as a part of their naval exercises. The FBI claims this theory of a training missile gone awry is ridiculous.

William Donaldson, an attack pilot who flew eighty-six combat missions over Vietnam and Laos and conducted numerous crash investigations, came out of retirement when he read that the NTSB had claimed that the jet fuel on Flight 800 caused the crash. He was on a mission to discover the truth.

He formed his own investigative committee with information leaked to him by dissidents inside the investigation and testimony from the former TWA pilot who was an engineer on the plane on its last successful flight.

After concluding his research, Donaldson gave a three-hour briefing on what he believed caused the crash of Flight 800. Donaldson's extensive evidence "proving" that a missile brought down Flight 800 included eyewitness testimony that he personally obtained. Al Gipe, a former navy gunnery officer, said he saw what looked like a 40mm tracer bullet streak up towards the plane until it exploded. Donaldson took this testimony and that of others and created a chart which plotted where each person was when they saw what seemed to be a missile and where the missile was. Connecting the dots, he showed the path of one missile that appeared to have been launched from about a mile offshore from the barrier island that runs along the southern coast of Long Island.

Donaldson also pointed out that the radar at the McArthur Airport on Long Island had recorded a ship three nautical miles to the south of the crash site. For it to be recorded on radar, its superstructure had to rise at least sixty feet above the water. Its size and speed ruled out a merchant ship. On radar, after the plane exploded, this ship raced out to sea instead of heading for the accident site to see if it could help anyone. Donaldson believed the ship on radar may have shot the missile that brought down Flight 800 then fled across the sea. This is the only one of four surface targets recorded on radar at the time of the crash that the FBI and NTSB say they have no knowledge of.

As for the flight data recorder information, Donaldson noted that the line "at 8:31 and 12 seconds" was deleted from the report that the NTSB released to be published. At 8:31 and 12 seconds the recorder data goes crazy. The plane violently pitched upward, switched from east to south in direction, and rolled on its right wing from 0 to 144 degrees, all in one second. Donaldson says "These numbers are indications of a tremendous blast. . . . In an instant, the typical passenger was displaced seventeen feet to the right, and twelve feet up." This is confirmed by the fact that according to the Suffolk County medical examiner's office, the cause of death for almost all of the 230 people aboard Flight 800 was a snapped neck.

Finally, Donaldson concluded that the tail section of the plane separated from the fuselage at about the same time the nose broke off. There was no evidence of fire or sooting to indicate that it broke off before the fuel tank exploded. This means that there could have been two high-energy explosions caused by two missiles—one striking near the front and one near the rear of the plane.

The FBI officially concluded that an accidental explosion of the center wing tank caused the crash of Flight 800. In November of 1997, the FBI announced its withdrawal from the Flight 800 crash investigation and released a fourteen-minute animated video simulation of the crash prepared by the CIA.

The tape explained how all the 244 witnesses to the crash saw the breakup of the Boeing 747 in the seconds after it exploded over the Atlantic Ocean, and not the explosion itself. The stream of light they saw that they thought was a missile hitting the plane was actually fuel burning as it leaked from the jet *after* its front part had already broken off.

The FBI officials also said witnesses heard the sound of the blast seconds later, since sound travels more slowly than light, making them believe they were seeing the beginning of the crash when in fact they were watching the end.

Ninety-six percent of the plane was recovered and examined by agents and scientists. Seven thousand interviews were conducted with workers at JFK and in Athens, Greece. Emergency calls and taped flight records were examined. "We left no stone unturned. In fact, we looked into every rock ten times," said Assistant FBI Director James Kallstrom when he explained that the crash was caused by an explosion in the plane's center fuel tank.

Although the NTSB has not yet released a final report, most investigators agree the explosion that caused the crash of Flight 800 emanated from the center fuel tank. And though there are many theories, exactly what caused this explosion remains a mystery.

A Potpourri of
New York Facts

Bare Facts about New York State

- New York has a total area of 53,989 square miles, 6,765 of which are water.
- According to a recent census, the population of New York is 18,169,000.
- On July 26, 1788, New York became the eleventh state.
- New York has sixty-two counties.
- The highest point is Mount Marcy in Essex County: 5,344 feet.
- The lowest point is sea level at the Atlantic Ocean.
- New York's state nickname is the Empire State, but sometimes it's called the Knickerbocker State for the knee breeches worn by Dutch settlers.

- New York's state nickname is attributed to George Washington, who supposedly predicted that the state would become the seat of the new empire.
- The state bird is the bluebird.
- The state fish is the brook trout.
- The state fossil, adopted in 1984, is *Eurypterus remipes.*
- The state baked good is the apple muffin.
- The state fruit is the apple.
- The state flower is the rose (no specific color).
- The state tree is the sugar maple.
- The state animal is the beaver.
- The state insect is the ladybug.
- The state gem is the garnet, mined in the Adirondack Mountains.
- The state motto is *Excelsior,* which means "ever upward." The motto was adopted in 1778 to indicate progress. It appeared on the state's first coat of arms.
- The state capital is Albany.
- The world's oldest chartered city is Albany.
- The unofficial state song is "I Love New York," by Steve Karmen.
- New York is a leader in the publishing, garment, and fur industries.
- In 1775, a year before the Declaration of Independence, 225 residents of Coxsackie signed their own declaration of independence.
- Ninety-two Revolutionary War battles were fought in New York, almost one third of the total number of battles fought.
- Samuel Wilson, a Troy meat packer, was know as Uncle Sam because he supplied the army with food during the War of 1812. His reputation spread until Uncle Sam became a U.S. symbol.
- New York got its name from the Duke of York and Albany, who received a patent to New Netherlands from his brother, Charles II.

• At Niagara Falls in upstate New York, 500,000 tons of water per minute plunge into the gorge.

Bare Facts about New York City

• It covers 304 square miles.

• It is the center of world finance and tourism.

• It is composed of five boroughs: The Bronx, Brooklyn, Manhattan, Queens, and Staten Island.

• It claims fifty islands; there are two thousand bridges in the city.

• The official name is The City of Greater New York.

• The official name of the Statue of Liberty is Liberty Enlightening the World.

• The city's official website is http://www.ci.nyc.ny.us.

• It has almost one million buildings.

• Its taxi drivers speak sixty different languages.

• Its official sister city is Tokyo, 10,870 miles away.

• It was the capital of the United States from 1783 to 1789.

• It has two major airports, Kennedy and LaGuardia.

• According to the 1990 census, 7.3 million people live in the city.

• It has 6,400 miles of streets.

• There are twenty million miles of telephone wires below the ground.

• Fort Tryon Park is the highest natural spot (248 feet) in Manhattan.

• It is called the Big Apple because jazz musicians thought of it as the biggest and juiciest gig they could get. Before it was known as the Big Apple, it was known as Gotham, Empire City, The City Beautiful, and The Big Town.

• Flags hanging outside the famous Waldorf Astoria Hotel in Manhattan indicate the foreign VIP's that are present inside.

- In Manhattan, odd-numbered streets run west and even-numbered streets run east.
- If a subway station displays a green globe, it is staffed twenty-four hours. If the globe is red, the station is closed.
- In NYC, Noho means north of Houston (pronounced by New Yorkers as House-ton) Street, and Soho means south of Houston Street.
- The Bronx Cheer is a loud, vulgar sound made by blowing across your tongue. It is used to express disgust at a professional sports player's performance.

Some famous New Yorkers include Billy Crystal, Priscilla Beaulieu Presley, Christopher Reeve, Jodie Foster, Arlo Guthrie, Robert Vaughn, William F. Buckley, Jr., Ed Sullivan, Jackie Gleason, Humphrey Bogart, James Cagney, Herman Melville, John Davison Rockefeller, Barbra Streisand, Michael Jordan, Neil Simon, Rod Serling, and Mario Puzo.

Little-known facts about New York City history

In the early twentieth century, **Roosevelt Island** in the East River was known as Blackwell Island, and it housed the insane, destitute, and imprisoned.

When explorer David Livingston was lost in Africa in 1871, the *New York Herald* dispatched Henry Stanley to find him and the famous words he uttered when he tracked him down were **"Dr. Livingston, I presume."**

One of the first concerts at Carnegie Hall was conducted by Peter Ilich Tchaikovsky in 1891.

In the Metropolitan Museum of Art you can find the entire Temple of Dendur from Ancient Egypt.

Louis Sullivan, the founder of modern architecture in America, designed the building at 65 Bleecker Street.

Scott Joplin, the famous composer, died in 1917 in a mental hospital on Ward's Island.

The Cyclone, Coney Island's famous wooden roller coaster ride, lasts one minute and fifty seconds.

The Hemlock Grove, all that remains of the forest that used to cover the city, is at the New York Botanical Garden in the Bronx.

Until 1686, when they were all killed, **wolves** still roamed the streets of New York.

Until 1934, **sheep grazed in the Central Park meadow.**

The **city's oldest museum** is the New-York Historical Society at Central Park West and 76th Street.

In 1917 and 1937, **two concrete tunnels** were opened. All water that flows into the city comes through these tunnels. To date, these tunnels have never been inspected. They carry sixty percent more water than they were originally designed to carry. Neither can be shut down because one tunnel could not bear all the weight of the other's water. Since the valves have never been closed, experts don't know if it is possible to turn them off, or to reopen them if they are closed. If tried, the city could lose its water supply. Construction on a third tunnel was started in 1970 and hopefully will be completed by the year 2020.

The battleship *Missouri,* one of the most famous ships ever built, and on whose deck the Japanese signed the surrender ending World War II, was built in the Brooklyn Naval Yard.

The **original Little Red Schoolhouse,** built in 1695, is currently the Voorlezer's House, on Staten Island.

The **most famous dropout** of Erasmus Hall High School in Brooklyn is chess champion Bobby Fisher.

Brooklyn sports fans were traumatized on October 8, 1957 when the Dodgers moved to Los Angeles.

Homing pigeons are trained in Maspeth, Queens.

In the 1930s and 40s **Robert Moses,** a parks commissioner and master builder, improved the city with new bridges, highways, parks, and beaches.

John Lennon fans can offer their respects to his memory at Strawberry Fields in Central Park, near West 72nd Street.

The prestigious **Pulitzer Prize** award was first given in 1917 in honor of local New York publisher Joseph Pulitzer.

The **poem by Emma Lazarus inscribed on the pedestal of the Statue of Liberty,** "Give me your tired, your poor . . ." was actually added after the statue was unveiled. The words have nothing to do with the statue's original purpose (see Chapter 15).

New York City's World Records and Firsts

Queens Museum has the world's largest scale model—the panorama depicts the five boroughs and their important buildings and natural features.

The Williamsburgh Savings Bank building in Brooklyn has the world's largest clock on top of it. Each of the clock's four sides has a diameter of twenty-seven feet.

Broadway in NYC is the longest city street in the world. It stretches 150 miles between Bowling Green in Manhattan to Albany, New York.

The **Verrazano Narrows Bridge** is the longest suspension bridge in the city and country: 54,260 feet long.

Gravesend, once a separate village in Brooklyn, was the first colony founded by a woman, Lady Deborah Moody, in 1643.

The first crossword puzzle appeared on December 2, 1913 in the *New York World.*

The first full-length talking picture, *Lights of New York,* opened on July 6, 1928 at the Strand Theater in Times Square.

The world's first flea circus opened on Broadway in 1835. It was billed as the "Extraordinary Exhibition of the Industrious Fleas."

The first radio sponsor was The Queensborough Realty Corporation on radio station WEAF in 1922.

The world's first hotel to have an elevator was the Fifth Avenue, in 1859.

The first free evening school for adults was established in College Point in 1868 at the Poppenhusen Institute.

Gertrude Ederle was the first woman to swim the English Channel. On August 6, 1926, she swam the thirty-five-mile-wide channel in fourteen hours and thirty-one minutes, beating the records set by men.

Charles Atlas, once a ninety-seven pound weakling, won the body-building title of the World's Most Perfectly Developed Man.

The *Guinness Book of World's Records*'s most versatile man, Ashrita Furman, lives in Queens, New York and holds more world records than anyone.

The *Guinness Book of World's Records*'s fastest talking female (and co-author of this book) Fran Capo lives in Queens, speaking at a rate of 603.32 words per minute.

New York University was the first college to field lacrosse, in 1877.

The very first stuffed Pooh Bear, Tigger, Piglet and Eeyore can be seen at Pooh Corner in the Donnell Library, at 20 West 53rd Street.

St. John the Divine is the largest cathedral in the city and in the world. It is located at Amsterdam Avenue at West 112th Street, in the Morningside Drive section of Manhattan. The nave of the Cathedral is 601 feet high.

The country's first Turkish bath was opened in Brooklyn in 1863.

The largest secondhand bookstore in the world, with eight miles of books, is the Strand Bookstore at Broadway and 12th Street.

The world's first science museum for the young was founded in 1899. It is the Brooklyn Children's Museum, at 145 Brooklyn Avenue.

Further Reading

Brett, Hy. *The Ultimate New York City Trivia Book*. Nashville, Tennessee: Rutledge Hill Press, 1997.

Callow, Alexander. *The Tweed Ring*. Oxford University Press: New York, 1965.

Frost, James and David Ellis, Harold Syrett, and Harry Carman, *A Short History of New York State*. Ithaca, New York: New York Historical Association in cooperation with Cornell University, 1957.

Furer, Howard. *A Chronological and Documentary History of New York from 1524-1970*. Dobbs Ferry, New York: Oceana Publications, 1974.

Gallager, John J. *The Battle of Brooklyn: 1776*. New York: Sarpendon Publishers, 1995.

Goodnough, David. *The Colony of New York*. New York: Franklin Watts, 1973.

Kammen, Michael. *Colonial New York: A History*. New York: Oxford University Press, 1975.

Kaplan, Stephen, and Roxanne Salch Kaplan. *The Amityville Horror Conspiracy*. Laceyville, PA: Belfry Books, 1995

Lankevich, George J. *American Metropolis: A History of New York City*. New York: New York University Press, 1998.

Moscow, Henry *The Book of New York Firsts* , Syracuse University Press, 1982/1995.

New-York Historical Society. 77th Street and Central Park West. (212) 873-3400.

Ritchie, Robert. *Captain Kidd and the War Against the Pirates*. Boston: Harvard University Press, 1986.

Sutton, Willie, with Edward Linn. *Where the Money Was*. New York: Viking Press, 1976.

White, Andrew W. "The Great Cardiff Giant." *Autobiography of Andrew White*. Chapter LVI. 1869.

Index

About the Authors

Fran Capo is a freelance writer and author of three books: *How to Get Publicity Without a Publicist; How to Break into Voiceovers;* and *Humor in Business Speaking.* She is also a stand-up comic, lecturer, and the *Guinness Book of World's Records's* Fastest Talking Female. This Queens College graduate has been on over 248 radio shows and 98 TV shows, including *Larry King Live, Entertainment Tonight,* and *Good Morning America,* and featured in numerous books, including *Chicken Soup for the Woman's Soul.* She created the first cybersitcom called "The Estrogen Files: Money, Men and Motherhood" at www.theestrogenfiles.net. She is the proud mother of Spencer Patterson (the world's youngest ventriloquist). Fran can be reached at her email address: FranCNY@aol.com or visit her website http://members.aol.com/franCNY/index.html.

Frank Borzellieri is a graduate of St. John's University, which he attended on a scholarship. He works as a journalist and editorialist and has been published in major publications such as *USA Today* and *Newsday.* His book, *The Unspoken Truth: Race, Culture and Other Taboos* was published by New Century Books. He is currently a columnist for the *Ledger-Observer* newspaper chain in New York City. Frank is the co-host of the television talk show *Democracy in Crisis* and has been profiled in the *New York Times, Washington Times, Daily News, New York Post, Newsday, National Review, Village Voice,* and many others. He has appeared on hundreds of television and radio programs, including *20/20, Geraldo Rivera, Ricki Lake,* and *Good Morning America.*